AF576425

TALES OF JAPAN

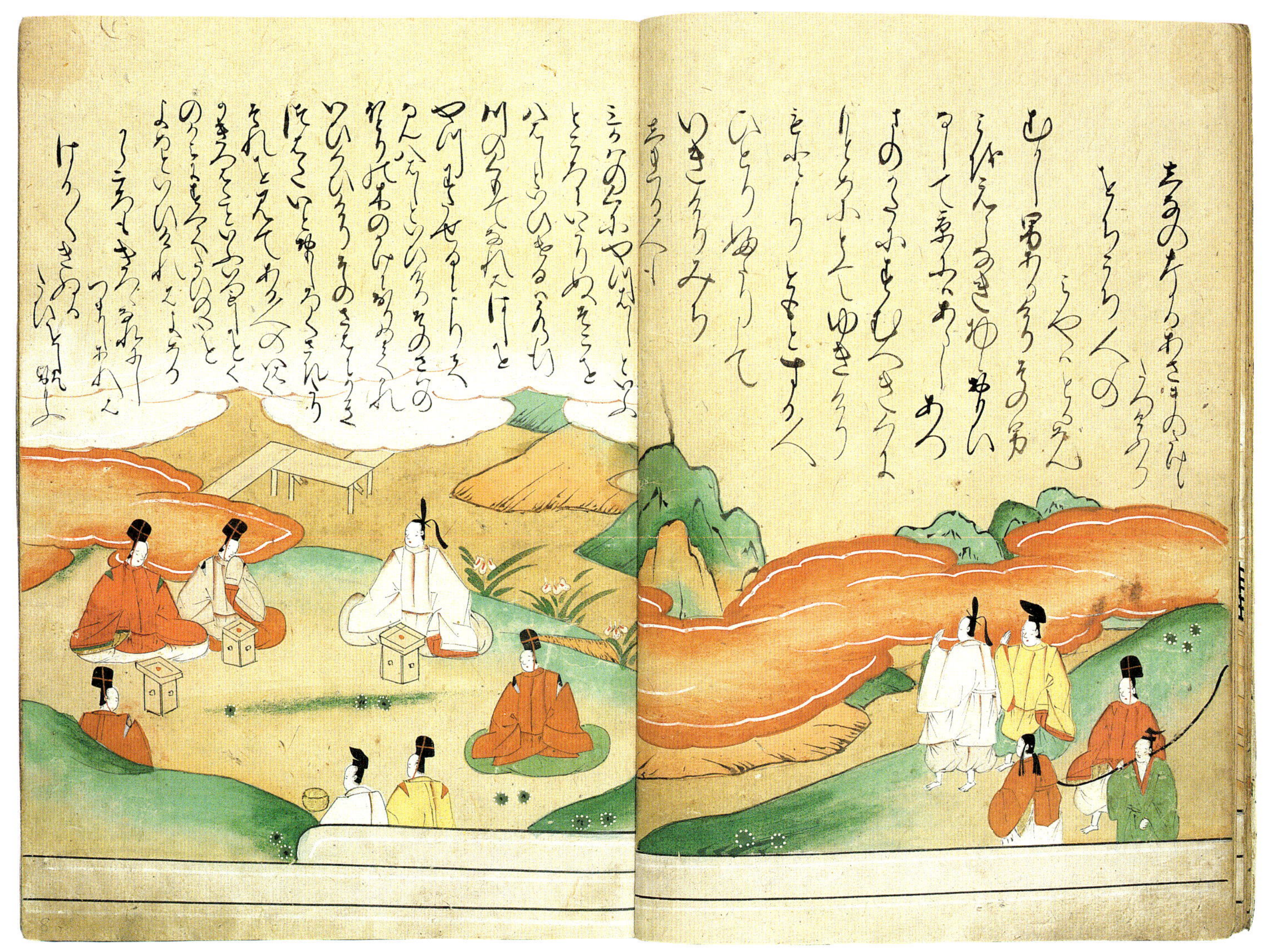

7.

TALES OF JAPAN

THREE CENTURIES
OF JAPANESE PAINTING
FROM THE
CHESTER BEATTY LIBRARY,
DUBLIN

ART SERVICES INTERNATIONAL
ALEXANDRIA, VIRGINIA
1992

Participating Museums

Indianapolis Museum of Art
Indianapolis, Indiana

Dayton Art Institute
Dayton, Ohio

Sunrise Museums
Charleston, West Virginia

Hood Museum
Dartmouth College
Hanover, New Hampshire

The exhibition is organized and circulated by Art Services International, Alexandria, Virginia.

Editor: Nancy Eickel
Designer: Judy Oser, Oser Design, Alexandria, VA
Photographers: Suntory Museum of Art, Tokyo
P.D.I., Dublin
Printed in Hong Kong by South China Printing Company

Cover: *Sanjūrokkasen Gajō* by Sumiyoshi Jokei (cat. no. 33)
Frontispiece: *Ise Monogatari* by an anonymous artist (cat. no. 7)

ISBN 0-88397-103-8

Library of Congress Cataloging-in-Publication Data

Ushioda, Yoshiko, 1931–
[Nihon no monogatarie. English]
Tales of Japan : Three centuries of Japanese painting from the Chester Beatty Library, Dublin / Yoshiko Ushioda.
p. cm.
Translation of: Nihon no monogatarie.
Exhibition catalog.
Includes bibliographical references.
ISBN 0-88397-103-8
1. Painting, Japanese—Kamakura-Momoyama periods, 1185–1600—Exhibitions. 2. Painting, Japanese—Edo period, 1600–1868—Exhibitions. 3. Chester Beatty Library—Exhibitions. I. Title. II. Title: Three centuries of Japanese painting from the Chester Beatty Library, Dublin.
ND1053.4.U8413 1992
759.952'074'74—dc20 92-15304
CIP

Contents

Acknowledgments

In our ongoing effort to acquaint American audiences with superb art collections from throughout the world, Art Services International is honored to present *Tales of Japan: Three Centuries of Japanese Painting from the Chester Beatty Library, Dublin.* The exquisite works housed in the Chester Beatty Library and Gallery of Oriental Art are little known beyond Dublin, and with this exhibition and catalogue, we hope to bring the Chester Beatty collection to the attention of a wide American audience. Because of their brilliance as paintings and their importance as historical records of Japanese culture, these colorful scrolls and illustrated albums deserve our careful attention and deep admiration.

The primary force behind this endeavor from its earliest stages has been Yoshiko Ushioda. As Japanese Curator of the collection and Guest Curator of this exhibition, Mrs. Ushioda has drawn from her years of research and familiarity with these works in choosing sixty-five key examples that highlight the breadth and beauty of Japanese painting. We are indebted to her for the enthusiasm, knowledge, and patience she has displayed throughout the development of this project.

We extend our special thanks to Dr. Michael Ryan, Director of the Chester Beatty Library, and Justice Brian Walsh, Chairman of the Board, for supporting the exhibition and ensuring its ultimate realization. Mrs. Roma S. Crocker, a valued Trustee of ASI, has been instrumental in this process, and we send her our heartfelt thanks for her assistance and encouragement. We are also pleased to acknowledge Dermot A. Gallagher, Irish Ambassador to the United States, and Takakazu Kuriyama, Japanese Ambassador, for recognizing the significance of this project and agreeing to serve as Honorary Patrons. Our respects extend as well to Eamonn McKee, Cultural Officer of the Irish embassy, and Kazuhiro Tajiri, Cultural Attaché of the Japanese embassy. We are most grateful for the cooperation they have shown us.

Sharing our enthusiasm for this exhibition and catalogue have been the directors and curators of the hosting museums. In particular we would like to acknowledge Bret Waller and Dr. James Robinson of the Indianapolis Museum of Art, Alexander Lee Nyerges and Clarence Kelley of the Dayton Art Institute, J. Hornor Davis IV of the Sunrise Museums, and Dr. Timothy Rub of the Hood Museum, Dartmouth College. Their participation has been invaluable, and it has been a distinct pleasure to collaborate with them and with their staffs.

Finally, it is a pleasure to express our sincere appreciation to the staff of Art Services International, in particular to Donna Elliott, Ana Lim, Susan Raines, and Douglas Shawn. Without their professionalism and dedication, this project would not have been realized.

Lynn Kahler Berg
Director

Joseph W. Saunders
Chief Executive Officer

Foreword

On behalf of the Trustees of the Chester Beatty Library, it gives me great pleasure to congratulate the organizers of the American tour of *Tales of Japan,* which comprises treasures of Japanese art from our collections. These were acquired by Sir Chester Beatty during and after his stay in Japan, where he spent several months in 1917. The Trustees are happy to know that this important part of their priceless collections will now be brought to the attention of the people of Chester Beatty's native country.

Alfred Chester Beatty (1875-1968) was an American of Irish, English, and Scottish ancestry. Born in New York, he studied at Princeton University, for which he always retained a deep affection, and at Columbia University, from which he graduated in 1898 with great distinction as a mining engineer. His profession enabled him to travel widely in the world, and his success may be judged by the fact that by 1917 he was already a millionaire. He became one of the world's greatest collectors of Islamic and Far Eastern art and also acquired many precious examples of the art of other cultures and civilizations, including that of the West.

In the 1950s, he came to reside in Ireland and brought with him his world-renowned collection. That he should choose to live in Ireland and locate his collections there has been described as the greatest single cultural event in Ireland this century. In 1957, the government of Ireland conferred upon him the unique distinction by making him the first honorary citizen of Ireland. When he died in 1968, he was given a state funeral. Both actions stand as fitting tributes to a prince of benefactors.

Through his last will he established the Trustees of the Chester Beatty Library and bequeathed to them his priceless collections, and the buildings in which they were housed, to hold in trust for the people of Ireland and beyond. The Trustees are deeply concious of the privilege and of the obligation of being the guardians of the Chester Beatty Collection and are most happy when the occasion arises, as it now does, to share the joy of this collection with others. We sincerely hope that the *Tales of Japan* exhibition will give great pleasure to those who visit it in different parts of the United States.

Justice Brian Walsh
Chairman
Chester Beatty Library

Sir Chester Beatty and His Japanese Collection

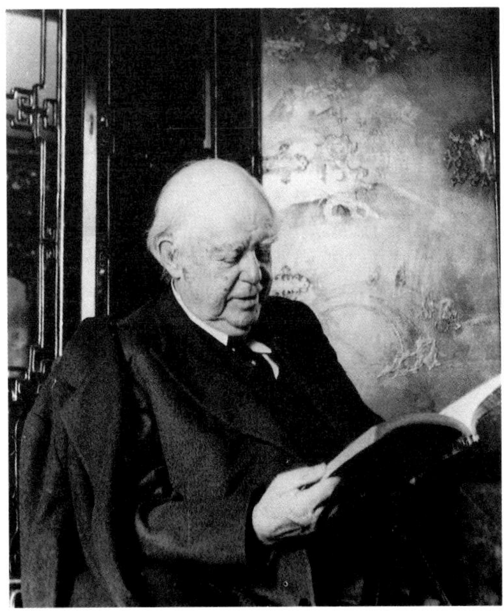

Sir Chester Beatty

One day in the early 1970s, the Far Eastern curator of the Chester Beatty Library in Dublin telephoned me, saying, "Would you come to the Library to meet a Japanese visitor who wants to see the *nara-ehon*?" In those days I was working at the Library for only a few hours a week helping to catalogue the Japanese woodblock prints, and we had very few Japanese visitors because the Library was little known even in Ireland. Our visitor was neither a scholar in fine art nor an art historian, but rather a professor of medieval Japanese literature. For this reason we wondered what the importance of the *nara-ehon* collection was that he had come so far to study it. The answer came several years later in August 1978 when, for the first time in history, an international and interdisciplinary symposium on *nara-ehon* took place at the Chester Beatty Library. The occasion was memorable not only in introducing the fine collection of Japanese art to the many scholars from different countries who participated in the symposium, but also in setting the seal on the importance of this remarkable collection of Japanese painted narrative scrolls and albums.

This impressive but largely unrecognized collection was assembled by Alfred Chester Beatty, who was born in New York in 1875. His paternal grandparents were both from Ireland. As a young boy, Chester Beatty became interested in mineral samples, and this encouraged him to pursue a career as a mining engineer. In 1898, he graduated from Columbia University School of Mining. He decided to head west and bought a one-way ticket to Denver, Colorado. His career began as a "mucker" (laborer in a mine), shoveling rock at the Kekionga Gold Mine in Boulder County. His pay was twenty-five cents an hour for a ten-hour day. Mining life was rough and dangerous, but courage and hard work paid off handsomely. Within ten years, Chester Beatty had made his way from mucker to foreman, supervisor to mine manager, mine owner to millionaire. He had, however, paid the price in terms of his health, and in 1910, suffering from silicosis, he was refused a life insurance policy. Despite such a modest start, this highly successful businessman amassed a phenomenal fortune, and by an irony of fate he lived to the age of ninety-four.

In 1914, Chester Beatty founded his own mining company, Selection Trust Limited. World War I delayed expansion of the enterprise, but during the 1920s the business surged forward to become a group of companies with interests in many countries, including Russia, the Gold Coast, and Sierra Leone. It was, however, in Northern Rhodesia (now Zimbabwe) and the Belgian Congo (now Zaire) that Chester Beatty's fortune was made when he dared to exploit the copper belt.

It was during this prosperous period that Chester Beatty built the greater part of his collection of Babylonian clay tablets, Egyptian papyri, painted miniatures from Persia, Turkey, and India, and other Islamic manuscripts. His interest in Oriental art was apparently first kindled as a young man in New York by his encounter with Chinese snuff bottles at an Oriental art dealer's shop called Yamanaka Shōkai. Enchanted by the rare and semiprecious stones and also by the beautiful colors of the bottles, he began to collect them with great enthusiasm from that time on.

Few records concerning Chester Beatty's early acquisitions of Japanese art remain, although we know that a collection of decorative art, *netsuke, inro,* lacquerware, and *tsuba* was assembled in his early days in New York, while his famous collection of Japanese woodblock prints was formed in the 1950s for him by the eminent English scholar Jack Hillier. It is no wonder, therefore, that the exceptional painted scrolls and albums discovered in 1963 by Barbara Ruch, now professor of Medieval Japanese Literature at Columbia University, were mistaken for an acquisition of his later years. We now realize that these treasures were purchased very early in Chester Beatty's career.

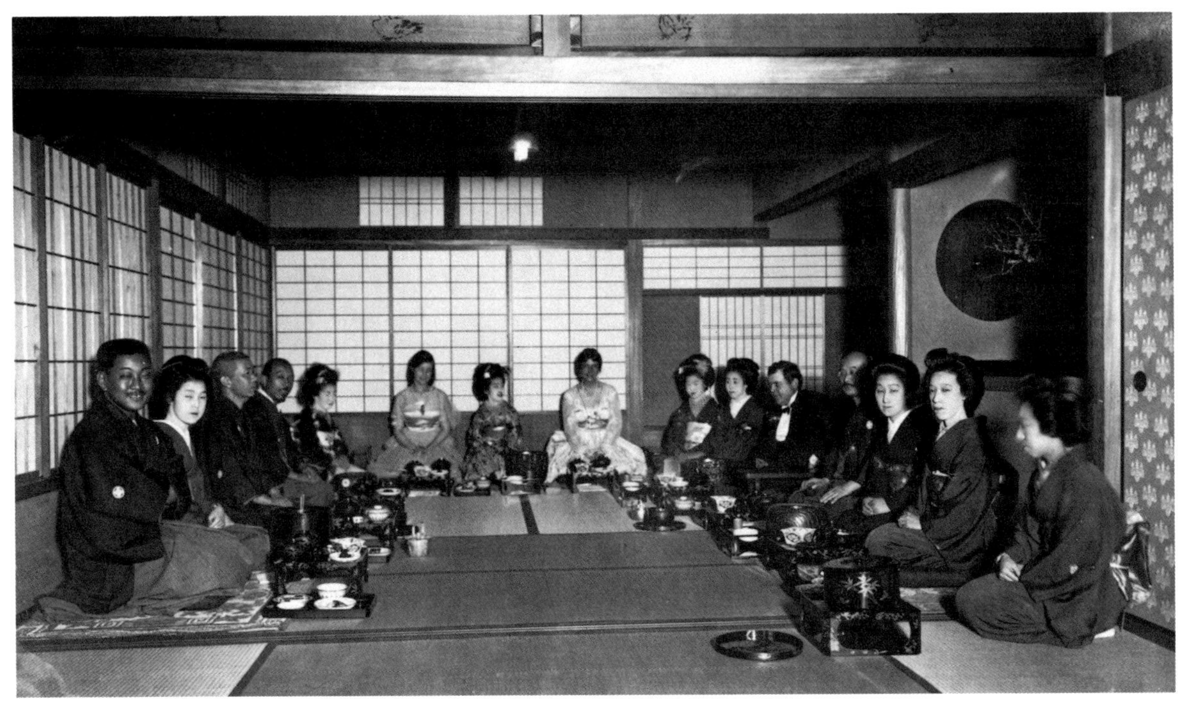

Sir Chester Beatty (fifth from right) in Osaka

In 1917, after suffering severely from pneumonia and Spanish influenza, Chester Beatty set out on a round-the-world sea voyage in the hope of regaining his health. That spring he made a stop in Japan where, as a good customer of Yamanaka Shōkai in New York, he was treated as an important guest and entertained by the head office of the firm. In fact, he spent a total of four months in Japan accompanied by his wife, daughter, a maid, and by an English-speaking guide, Okita Yatarō . It was this trip that fueled Chester Beatty's fascination with the East.

While I was researching his archives prior to the symposium of 1978, I found an old file that contained notes of Chester Beatty's visits to antique dealers in Kyoto, Nara, Osaka, and Yokohama, together with details of his purchases and application forms for shipments to New York. Also included was a photograph of a dinner party hosted by Yamanaka Sadajirō of Yamanaka Shōkai in Osaka in honor of Chester Beatty. From these archives it was confirmed that during his stay in Japan, Chester Beatty purchased many *nara-ehon* and other painted albums and scrolls of the late Muromachi and Edo periods. In their coloring, *nara-ehon* strongly resemble the miniatures of Persia, Armenia, and India, which date from almost the same period. Perhaps for this reason Chester Beatty collected these manuscripts, for they reflect his personal taste for jewel-like colors.

Chester Beatty certainly did not collect them from an art historian's point of view. As a scientist and mining engineer himself, and of course as a foreigner, he undoubtedly was interested in Japanese historial records and documentary materials. Among these are the paintings commissioned at the time of the famine of 1837 (the eighth year of the Tempō period), which not only show desperate scenes of starvation but also illustrate the happy results of the good harvest that followed in 1839 (the tenth year of the Tempō period). Both scrolls were painted by Kino Yūbi (cat. no. 48). Similarly, the Ansei earthquake of October 2, 1855, was meticulously depicted on a paper scroll commissioned by Prince Konoe soon after the terrible event (cat. no. 49). The work begins with colorful scenery of maple trees and a peaceful night in Edo. Then, after a significant blank portion that symbolizes the earthquake, the scenes of disaster commence. Collapsed houses, people running about in confusion, large and small fires, and dead bodies and coffins are all realistically depicted. Soon after the disaster, people start the work of re-building their sheds and cottages, using partly burnt screens or sliding doors, and they clear and tidy the streets. Amazingly, the devastated city of Edo is quickly restored to a peaceful metropolis once again.

Another angle of the documentary scrolls is the portrayal of the everyday life of the Dutch merchants who were confined to their factory on the island of Dejima in Nagasaki (cat. no. 52). The minutely executed paintings on silk convey the wonder and deep curiosity about foreigners then felt by the people of Japan.

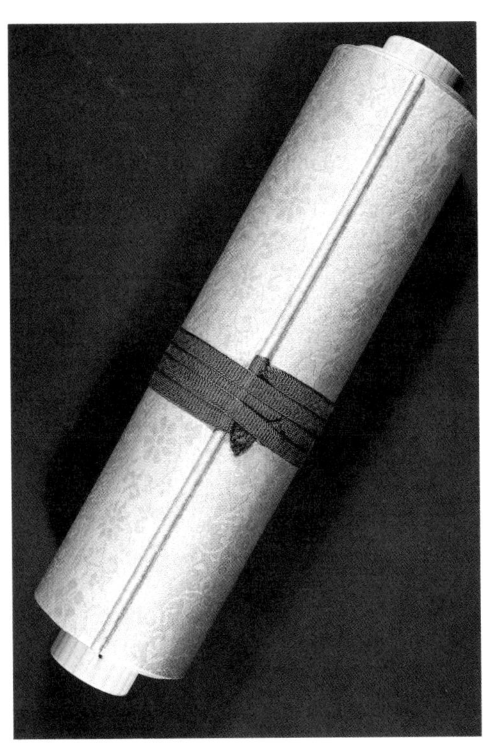

36. The scroll of *Tohi Zukan* rolled up

Tohi Zukan, a scroll of views in and around Kyoto painted by Sumiyoshi Jokei, illustrates street scenes and the prosperous lives of the people of Kyoto and its suburbs in the seventeenth century (cat. no. 36). Japanese historial records are further documented by an unusual series of scrolls that meticulously delineate the entire process by which gold was mined and minted in nineteenth-century Japan (cat. no. 51). As Chester Beatty was a mining engineer himself, this subject must have been of particular interest to him.

As with many foreign collections of Japanese art, the Chester Beatty Library is undoubtedly famous for its *ukiyo-e* collection. Although not as extensive in quantity, the *ukiyo-e* is of the finest quality (see cat. nos. 56-65). Jack Hillier, a leading *ukiyo-e* scholar, was commissioned by Sir Chester Beatty in the mid-1940s to begin assembling a fine collection for him. From the various written comments regarding Chester Beatty's acquisition of *ukiyo-e,* it is obvious that he always emphasized quality over famous names. He wrote to his librarian at the time, "I am satisfied, and the policy I want to pursue . . . is to back our joint judgement on quality and forget all about the artists. I saw a man here who had a complete set of Mt. Fuji views by Hokusai. Many of these were in a very poor condition and I would not have cared to own them." Sir Chester Beatty clearly put quality of condition before rarity, age, value, and artistic or aesthetic merit. His *ukiyo-e* collection was formed largely in the 1950s when he moved to Ireland.

Following the victory of the Labor Party in the British General Election of 1945, Chester Beatty began to feel uncomfortable in the country for which he had worked so hard during the Second World War as Winston Churchill's minerals expert. He was discouraged by the proliferation of bureaucracy, regimentation, and controls. By then, his son had lived in an Irish countryhouse in County Kildare, and Chester Beatty himself investigated the possibility of moving to Ireland. By the time he actually settled in Dublin in the 1950s, he possessed a large and excellent collection of Japanese scrolls and albums. To complete his Japanese collection, he was anxious to acquire a large number of fine prints and to buy works by as many of the *ukiyo-e* masters as possible.

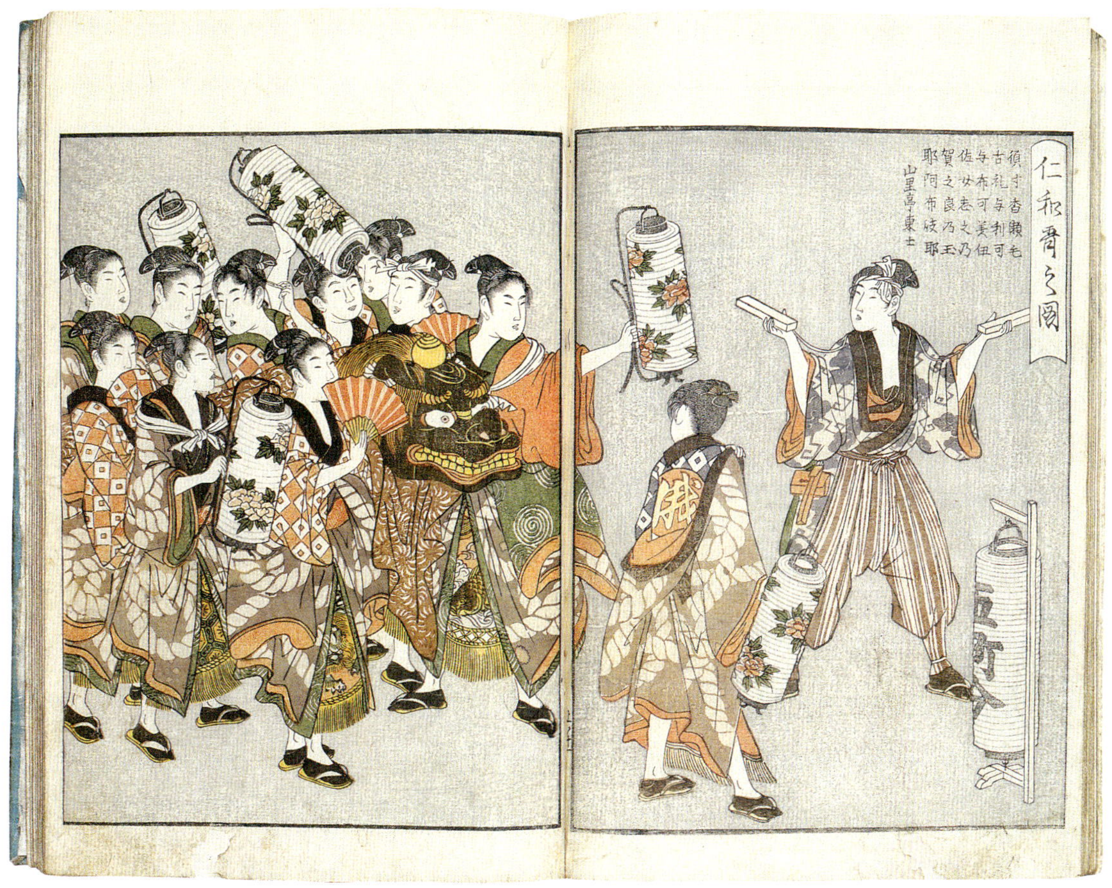

57.

Chester Beatty's friend and publisher, Wilfred Merton, spotted the Cooper Collection of *ukiyo-e* on the London market early in 1954. Basil Gray, then an Oriental scholar at the British Museum, thought the Cooper Collection outstanding, and he advised its purchase despite the high asking price. (The figure was by no means outrageous, since it included the privilege of owning this fine collection.) Jack Hillier also thought the Cooper Collection was of very high quality. So in May of that year, Chester Beatty bought the collection of 450 prints.

Jack Hillier recalled that Sir Chester Beatty would often refuse an excellent and extremely rare print because he considered it to be unhealthy, grubby, or dirty. In this sense, Hillier argued that Chester Beatty put pristine condition before artistic importance and rarity.

> I think people overlooked the question of the *surimono,* but there are arguments about the *surimono*—that they are a sort of miniature art, perhaps too elaborate, and they have not got the fine qualities of the larger prints. On the other hand, they are very charming, and they represent a very high position in skilled block printing, and the original was done by very very fine artists, particularly Hokusai. I think as time goes on they will be very much appreciated.

Surimono literally means "a printed object." During the 1760s, the term began to be applied to a new form of woodblock print whose popularity lasted well into the nineteenth century. These were privately commissioned prints, published in a limited edition for distribution among an intimate circle of friends or associates. Most *surimono* fall into one of two categories: those that commemorate a special event, and those that combine a picture with verse. Both types incorporate a written text. One of the finest qualities of *surimono* lies in the extraordinary subtlety with which the artist employs his imagery to complement the content of the text. Together, picture and words yield a richer experience than either could create independently. The Chester Beatty collection of *surimono* has indeed become one of the finest and most comprehensive in Europe, if not the world.

Prior to his death in 1968, Sir Chester Beatty demonstrated his intelligence and vision by bequeathing his immense collection of art to the Irish people. I hope, as indeed Sir Chester Beatty wished, that his collection will continue to provide a wealth of material for scholars of Japanese art and will serve as a valuable resource for those interested in Japanese culture and history. ❖

Painted Scrolls and Albums of the Pre-modern Period

The history of Japanese painted scrolls and albums may be traced to its earliest roots in the copying of Chinese paintings, an outgrowth of Japan's cultural origins in China. The oldest surviving Japanese painting—a scroll depicting the life of Buddha, which dates from the Nara period (645–794)—reflects the country's Chinese ties and its adoption of Buddhism in the sixth century. In the Heian period (794–1185), however, there appeared painted scrolls depicting Buddhist stories and the histories of traditional events, as well as stories and diaries on non-religious themes, all of which were well accepted among the aristocracy of the time. Well-known examples of valuable scrolls from this period include *The Tale of Genji;* the painted scroll of the origin of Shigisan, a temple in the Nara district; and the painted scroll of Ban Dainagon, a chief councilor of state. Towards the end of the Heian period, the histories of various Buddhist temples and shrines, together with biographies of some of their high priests, were produced as scrolls, which became popular among people of the ordinary classes in the Kamakura (1185–1333) and Muromachi (1333–1573) periods.

The Kamakura period is generally considered to be the most productive in the history of Japanese scroll painting, both in terms of quantity and quality. In the years following the six decades of upheaval that marred the fourteenth century, this prolific trend continued well into the Muromachi period, which saw the birth of a new style of painting that greatly differed from the refined elegance of the earlier aristocratic *yamato-e* style (literally, Japanese painting). The new style had much greater appeal for the general populace, since the paintings, such as *The History of Hasedera Temple, The History of Hachiman Shrine,* and *The Origin of Tenjin Shrine,* were based on the shared religious beliefs of the common people. In addition, this period saw the emergence of popular novels whose heroes and heroines were drawn from the ordinary classes, as in the theme of *Bunshō no Sōshi,* a poor salt-maker who becomes a rich man (cat.

no. 21). For the first time the lives of the common people were seen as worthy subjects for narrative treatment, a trend that may have come to be reflected in the painted scrolls and albums of the time.

Nevertheless, in the pre-modern period, which stretched for nearly three hundred years from the late Muromachi to the end of the Edo period (ca. 1573–1868), this relatively simple style of painting was gradually replaced by a newer kind characterized by an increasing formality. People and objects came to be depicted with great accuracy and attention to detail. (Compare the simple beauty of *The Tale of Ise* [cat. no. 7] with the stylization of *The Tale of Genji* [cat. no. 1].) This pre-modern *yamato-e* was quite different again from the traditional variety that had flourished during the Heian and Kamakura periods. The new *yamato-e* paintings depicted landscape and scenes from popular stories and from daily life in a manner that sharply contrasted to that of Chinese landscape painting. All the same, artists of the Kanō school, which was most closely associated with the Chinese style of painting, were also able to produce paintings in the richly colored and sophisticated style of the pre-modern *yamato-e* as customarily practiced by the artists of the Tosa and Sumiyoshi schools.[1] Such *yamato-e* paintings were similarly produced by painters living and working in the temples, as well as by amateur artists.

It was also during this pre-modern period that short stories known as *otogi zōshi* came to be widely read. Roughly translated, the term denotes "tales told by a companion." According to Murase Miyeko, the word *otogi* originally referred to the practice of telling stories to keep away evil spirits at dusk or to allay feelings of loneliness at bedtime.[2] Narrowly defined, however, the term *otogi zōshi* relates to a group of twenty-three short stories written during the Muromachi period and published in the early eighteenth century under this name. Appealing largely to the tastes of women and children, most of these stories were lavishly illustrated.

Color illustrations rich in detail were likewise a feature of Kōwaka Mai, texts of a form of musical drama whose themes were mainly drawn from fourteenth-century war stories, which appealed chiefly to those among the warrior class (see cat. no. 27). The classics too were produced as painted scrolls and albums during this period, with works such as *The Tale of Genji* (cat. nos. 1–6), *The Tale of Ise* (cat. no. 7), and *The Tale of the Bamboo Cutter* (cat. no. 8) undoubtedly attracting wide readership.

Furthermore, this period saw a gradual shift in emphasis and productivity from illustrated scrolls to albums, with the painted images in the albums following a pattern of stylistic evolution similar to that of the scrolls, that is, progressing from the less refined and less sophisticated towards the more detailed and decorative. (Compare, for example, the scroll of *The Tale of Genji* [cat. no. 1] and the fifty-four volumes of the same title [cat. no. 2].) The culmination of this development was *kazaridana bon,* luxurious illustrated albums designed to be placed on ornamental shelves usually in or alongside the *tokonoma,* or special alcove, in the house, and often forming part of a wealthy bride's wedding trousseau. In terms of splendor and magnificence, however, such albums could not compete with painted scrolls that illustrate the same subjects.

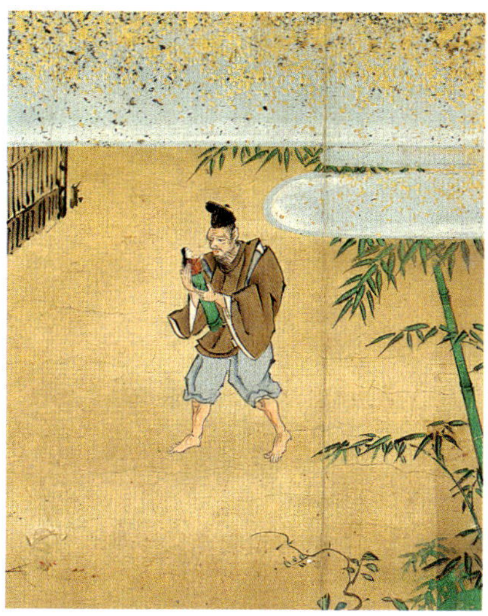

8. The bamboo cutter returns with the Shining Princess

The Chester Beatty collection contains many of these kinds of pre-modern scrolls and albums, all of which are of high quality and are exceptionally well preserved. One outstanding example is the three-volume set of *The Tale of Ise,* dating from the Momoyama period (1573–1603; cat. no. 7). The albums are painted in bright colors, a vivid orange and green being especially prominent, with clearly delineated figures portrayed admiring flowers, composing poems, or strolling in the mountains in simple but lyrical compositions. Of particular interest is the fact that the texts are written in the stylized clouds above the various illustrations. The integration of text with illustration is considered to be a development of the style of painted scrolls and albums of the Muromachi period (1333–1573) and is sometimes referred to as *konarae,* or the early *nara-e* style.

The pictorial representation of literary works, a key aspect of Japanese art, is richly realized in *nara-ehon.* Scenes are interpreted from classical literature, myths and legends, popular and historical events, tales of battles, and the history of temples. The terms *nara-e* and *nara-ehon,* meaning "nara picture" and "nara picture book," respectively, are somewhat difficult to define and are of uncertain origin and intent, although they were probably coined in the early part of this century. The vagueness of the terms may have been due to the general lack of scholarly interest in the works to which they were loosely applied. Today, *nara-ehon* refers to a group of illustrated works of literature hand-produced in either book or scroll format and dating from the fifteenth to the eighteenth century in Japan. According to scholars, *nara-ehon* were created not only in the Nara region but also in the areas of Kyoto and Osaka, usually to commemorate special occasions or to be given as wedding dowries and New Year gifts. Almost all these works are unsigned and were generally executed by anonymous artists from these regions. In later years they were so little valued that many left Japan and are now held mostly in foreign collections, such as that of the New York Public Library and the Chester Beatty Library in Dublin, Ireland.

These albums and scrolls are usually distinguished by the copious use of gold ink and foil, and thickly applied bright colors, as well as by the charmingly naive treatment of figures and landscape. The sheer vividness of the colors often makes up for this lack of subtlety in technique. One further outstanding characteristic of *nara-e* illustration is the use of mists and stylized clouds to frame scenes and to create decorative effect. Although criticized as technically somewhat amateur, *nara-ehon* succeed in affecting the viewer powerfully and directly.

One of the finest examples of *nara-ehon* in the Chester Beatty collection is the only extant copy of *Yoshitsune's Invasion of Hell* (cat. no. 14), which offers an interesting storyline and illustrations that are

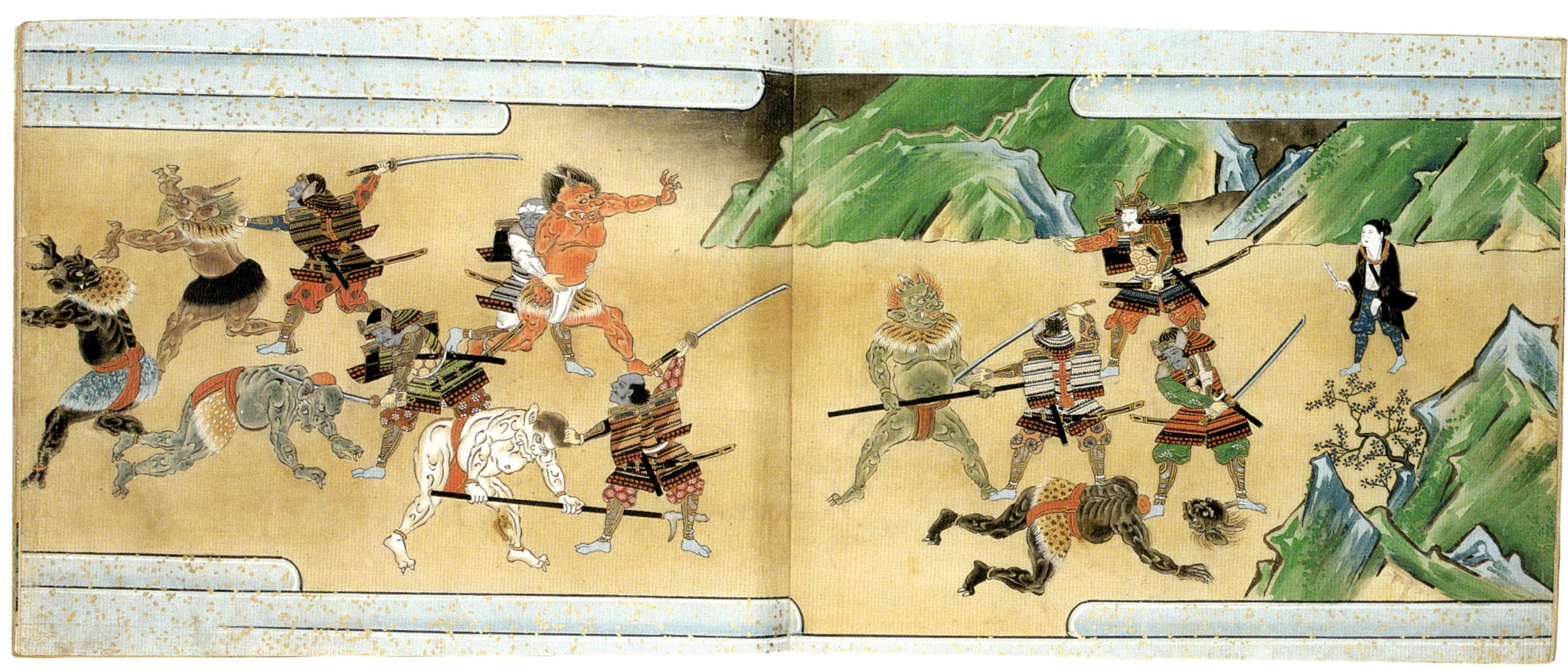

14. Yoshitsune invades Hell, with the ascetic watching

unsophisticated in manner. In addition to this masterpiece are the remarkable scrolls entitled *The Tale of Muramatsu* and attributed to the artist Iwasa Matabei (cat. no. 26). Also included is the only surviving scroll of the medieval tale of the hero Asahina (cat. no. 16) and *Mai no Hon* (cat. no. 27), an elegant depiction of a musical play and said to be one of the finest set of painted scrolls produced in the Edo period. The story of the warrior hero Benkei, as told in *The Tale of Musashibō Benkei* (cat. no. 12), proved very popular in the Muromachi and Edo periods. Many painted scrolls and albums on the subject of the monk's strange life and his relationship with his master Minamoto Yoshitsune, a famous war lord, were most likely produced during this time. The Chester Beatty scrolls depicting this tale are among the oldest and finest in existence. With its combination of brilliant colors, fast moving action, and realistic portrayal of human figures and expressions, the style of painting belongs to neither the Kanō nor the Tosa schools, but instead resembles the manner practiced by the amateur artists of the Nara and Osaka regions.

These introductory remarks have been necessarily brief and such an account cannot of course do justice to the paintings themselves. It is to be hoped that *Tales of Japan* will offer a welcome opportunity for American audiences to discover the art historial importance of the painted scrolls and albums of the pre-modern period of Japan. ❖

Author's Note

For the research and compiling of this catalogue text I am indebted to many scholars in Japan who provided me with valuable assistance when I was working on a Japanese version of this catalogue a few years ago. The latter was of course written in Japanese for the Japanese public, and consequently there was little need to explain well-known Japanese legends and literary classics. On this occasion, I have made extensive revisions and additions to the content to incorporate more in the way of background information for those unfamiliar with these elements of Japanese culture. I am sure that these beautiful works will speak for themselves and will offer many hours of pleasure and thought to the appreciative viewer.

Also, I wish to thank my daughter Ema for correcting, improving, and typing the entire manuscript for me, for without her help this catalogue would certainly not have been produced on time.

Chronology of Art Periods

Heian period	794–1185
Kamakura period	1185–1333
Muromachi period	1333–1573
Momoyama period	1573–1615
Edo period	1615–1868

Notes to the Catalogue

Titles of works are given in Japanese, followed by an English translation. Japanese personal names have been written, according to Japanese convention, with the family name first, followed by the given name. Dimensions appear in centimenters; height (H) precedes length (L) precedes width (W). CBJ refers to the Chester Beatty Japanese collection. Numbers in parentheses refer to the Sorimachi catalogue.[3]

Catalogue of Works

1.

Genji Monogatari Emaki

(The Tale of Genji)

Anonymous

1688

Four scrolls; ink, color, and gold on paper

I: H 45.5 L 1386; II: H 45.5 L 1275;

III: H 45.5 L 1274; IV: H 45.5 L 1393

CBJ No. 1126 (46)

The Tale of Genji was written by Lady Murasaki Shikibu (ca. 973–1030) while she was a lady-in-waiting at the imperial court. The story is set in the Heian period (794–1185) and concerns the life and loves of Prince Genji. The fifty-four-chapter story, noted for its grand scale and tightly knit plot embracing over four hundred characters, is still one of the most celebrated masterpieces in Japanese literature.

This particular set of four scrolls, called *Genji Kotobae,* is composed of fifty-four paintings in full color, each of which is accompanied by a chapter heading and a brief extract from the text of the novel. The text consists either of a poem or a prose excerpt appropriate to the subject of the painting. The calligraphy inscribed on the scrolls is the work of twenty-seven different calligraphers, each of whom provided the text extracts for two chapters. The names of these calligraphers, together with their official titles at court, are given on a separate paper scroll with the title "Mokuroku." Assuming that the writing was done during the period when these calligraphers held the titles specified on the list, the four scrolls were made between January 26 and December 26, 1688. Since all the texts selected for inclusion concern a happy event of some kind, these scrolls may have been commissioned for a special purpose, probably to mark the wedding of a daughter of a high-ranking court noble.

The names of the painters are unknown, but it is likely that the paintings were done either at the same time as the calligraphy or shortly thereafter. The paintings themselves are not particularly noteworthy, but the artists do appear to have been influenced by the Chinese school of painting, which is evident in the use of ink in these subtle images.

In general, the work resembles that of the artist Sumiyoshi Jokei (1631–1705), whose *Tale of Genji* painting was inscribed by fifty-four different calligraphers of courtier rank, headed by Emperor Reigen. Since the first three calligraphers to have inscribed the Chester Beatty scroll were all related to Emperor Reigen, this reinforces the possibility that the work was commissioned by a wealthy patron of high rank, as does the exceptionally large format of the scrolls with their display of rich colors and gold.

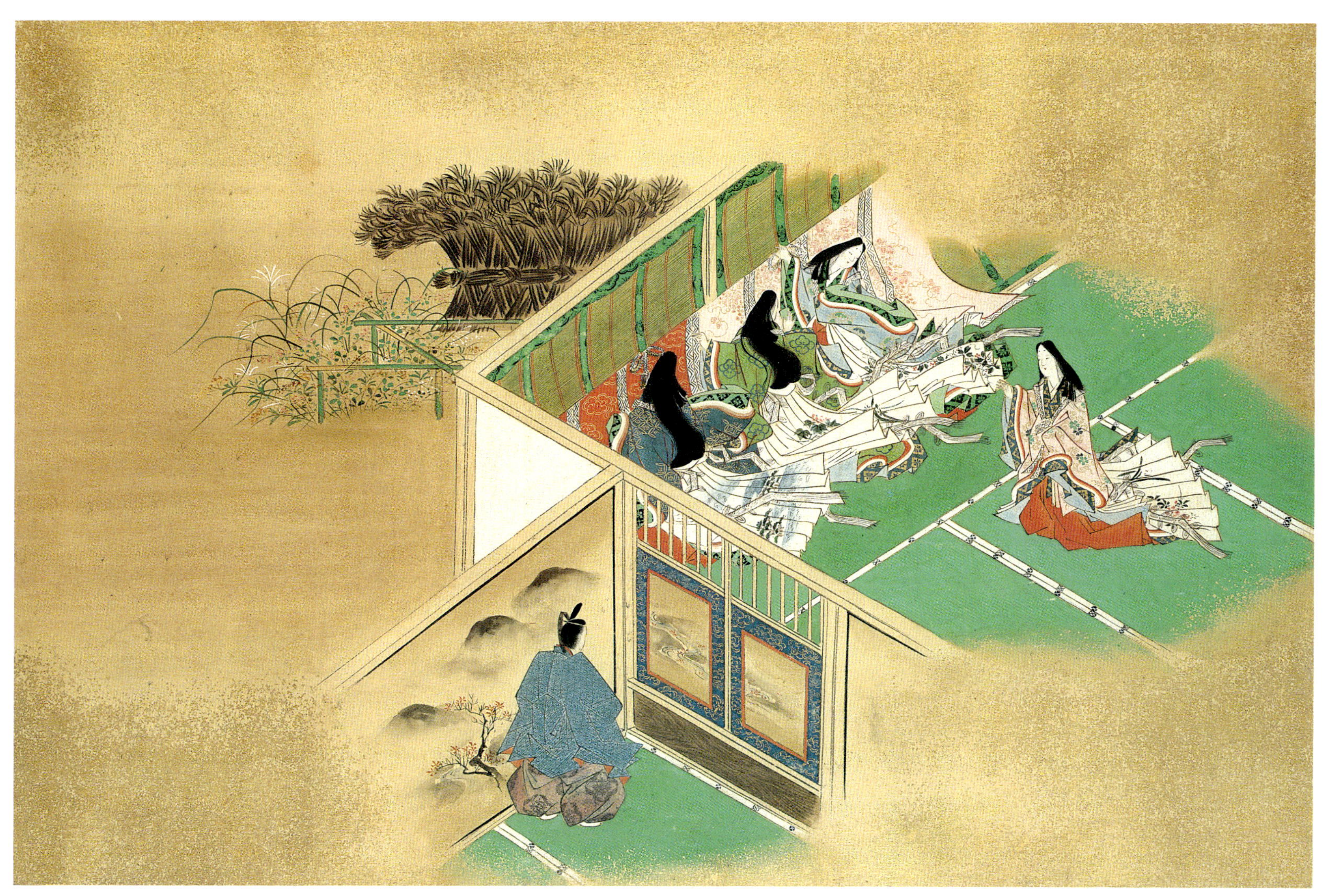

1. Prince Yugiri peeps through a screen after a stormy night (chapter 28, "Nowaki," The Typhoon)

2.

Genji Monogatari

(The Tale of Genji)

Anonymous

Middle of 17th century, Edo period

54 volumes; ink, colors, and gold on paper

H 23.5 L 17 (each)

CBJ No. 1038 (31)

These illustrated, handwritten albums were favored as dowry gifts for the daughters of rich famillies in the Edo period (1615–1868). This particularly good example of *nara-ehon* possesses an unusually large number of miniature paintings that are rich in jewel-like colors with gold ink and leaf. The calligraphy, in Kana script, is also of fine quality, but it is of the standard cursive style and was not executed by any notable calligrapher. Each volume contains a complete chapter with the full text and a selection of paintings that illustrate appropriate scenes from the tale.

The fifty-four volumes are preserved in their original black lacquer cabinet, which is decorated with gold and silver decorations *(maki-e)*. The title of each chapter is written in gold ink on the cabinet drawers. The set was undoubtedly produced for a rich feudal lord's daughter as part of her wedding dowry.

In all aspects, this is an outstanding synthesis of Japanese craftsmanship. The miniatures, calligraphy, bindings, and lacquered cabinet combine to make this set a remarkable composition and a delight to admire and read.

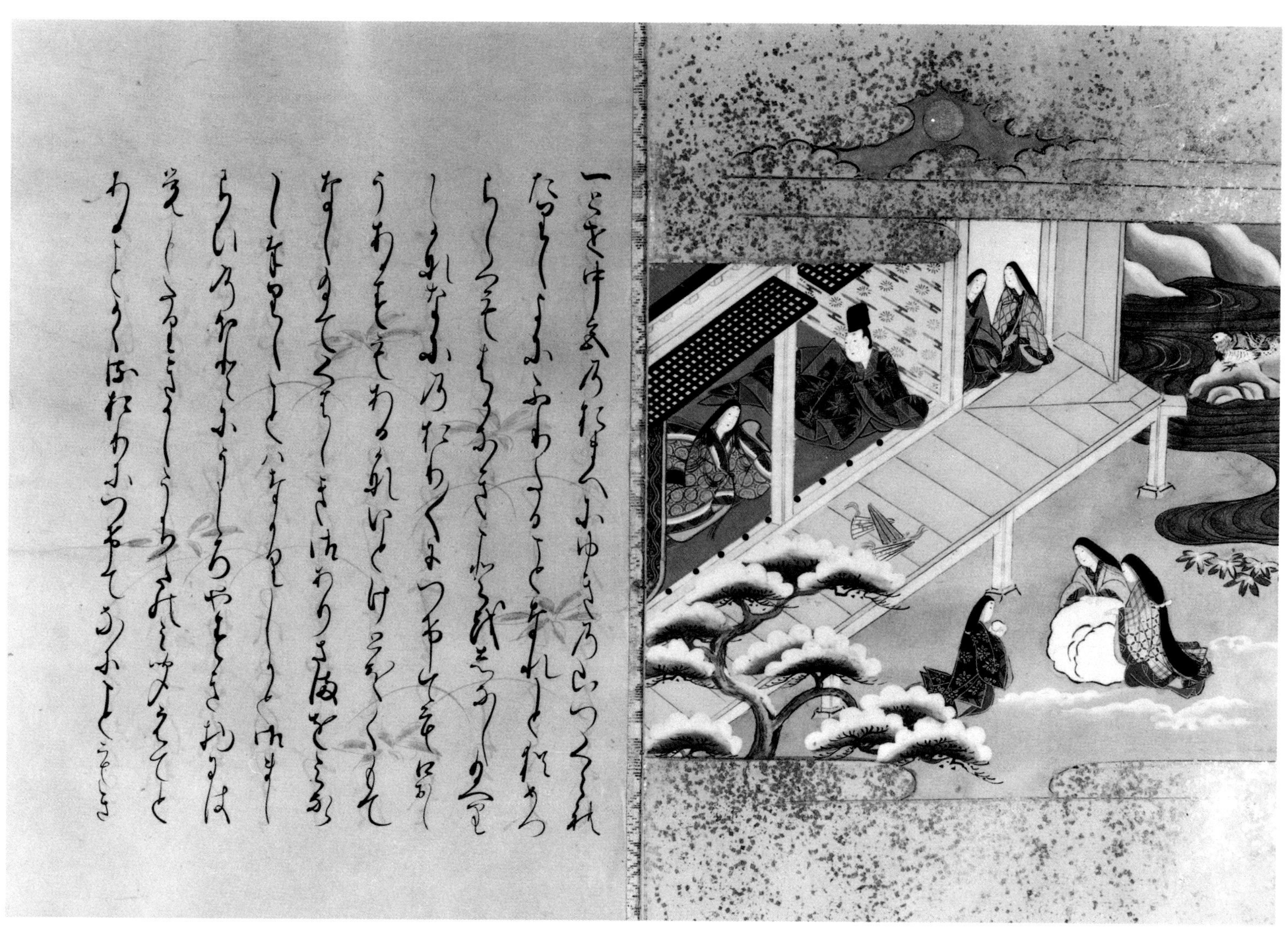

2. Prince Genji and Murasaki converse, as children roll a snowball outside (chapter 20, "Asagao," The Morning Glory)

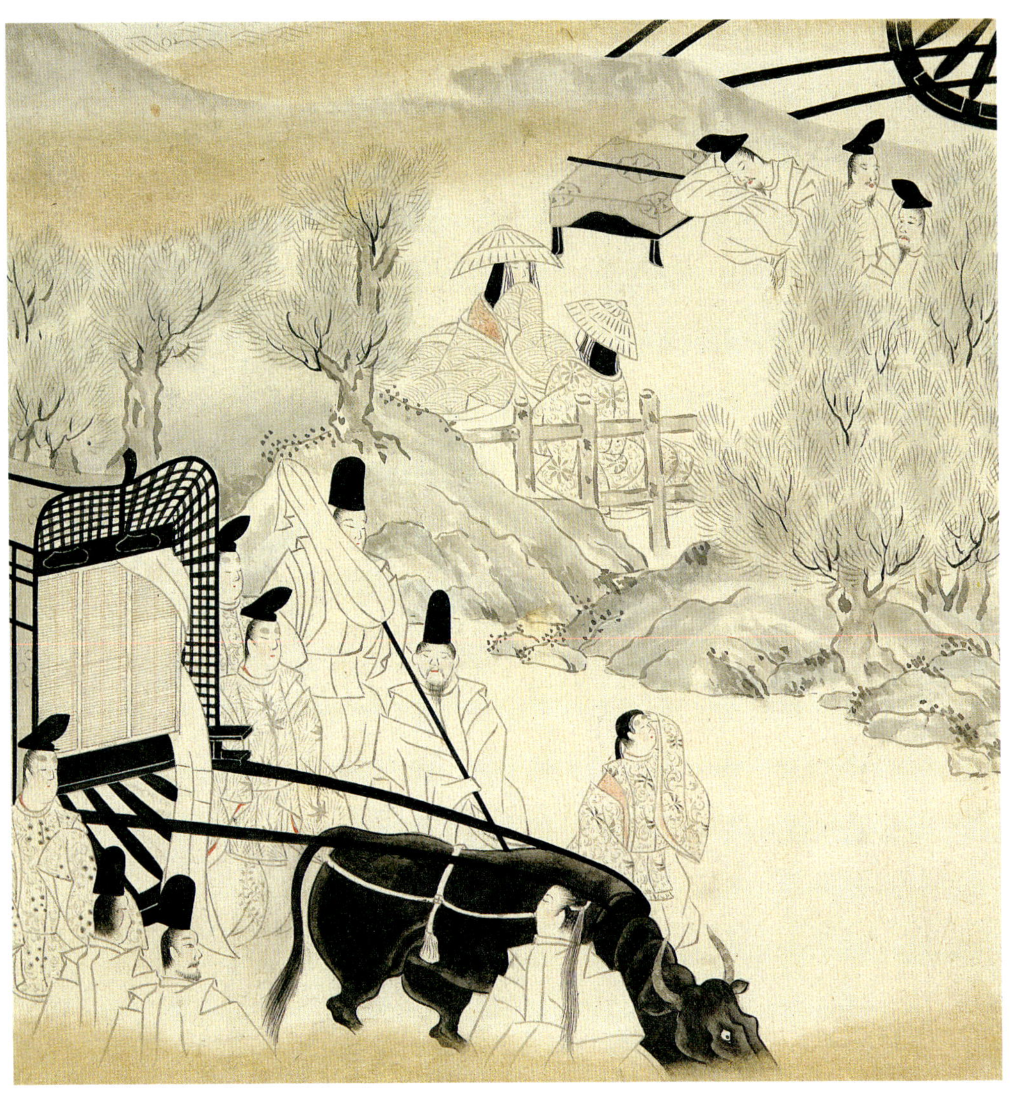

3. Prince Genji passes by Utsusemi, the lady of the locust shell, in a carriage (chapter 16, "Sekiya," The Gatehouse)

3.

Genji Monogatari Gajō

(The Tale of Genji)

Anonymous

Middle of 17th century, Edo period

One album; ink, colors, silver, and gold on paper

H 23 W 21.3

CBJ No. 1043 (49)

Although all the paintings seem to represent scenes from *The Tale of Genji,* the first seven paintings differ completely in style from the remaining twenty-three. The first seven are typical of *nara-ehon* Genji pictures executed in bright colors with copious use of gold ink and foil. The figures are extremely small yet richly expressive of individual character. The remaining paintings are in fine *hakubyō* (literally, white drawing), a kind of grisaille with faint touches of gold and red colors, composed in a highly refined and elegant manner.

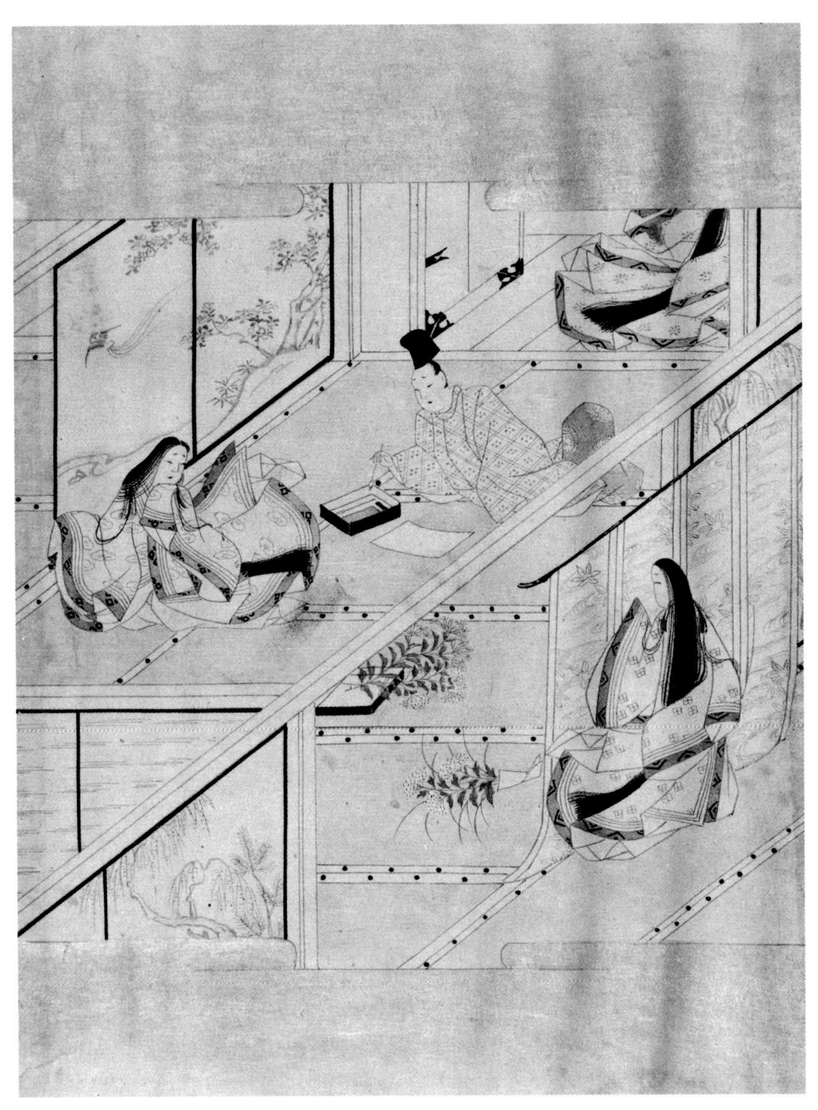

4. Prince Genji assists Princess Akashi in writing a poem to her mother (chapter 23, "Hatsune," The First Warbler)

4.

Genji Monogatari Gajō

(The Tale of Genji)

Anonymous

Middle of 17th century, Edo period

One album; ink, light colors, and gold on paper

H 27.2 W 20.5

CBJ No. 1051 (50)

The twenty-four paintings are in refined *hakubyō* style with faint touches of colors. The use of stylized mist and clouds interspersing scenes and creating a decorative effect is typical of *nara-ehon*. Although the format and composition of these paintings are similar to those of standard *nara-ehon*, the genre of *hakubyō* painting is significantly different. The paintings are more refined and tasteful than *nara-ehon* and would seem to be intended for somewhat more aristocratic patrons.

There are no accompanying texts.

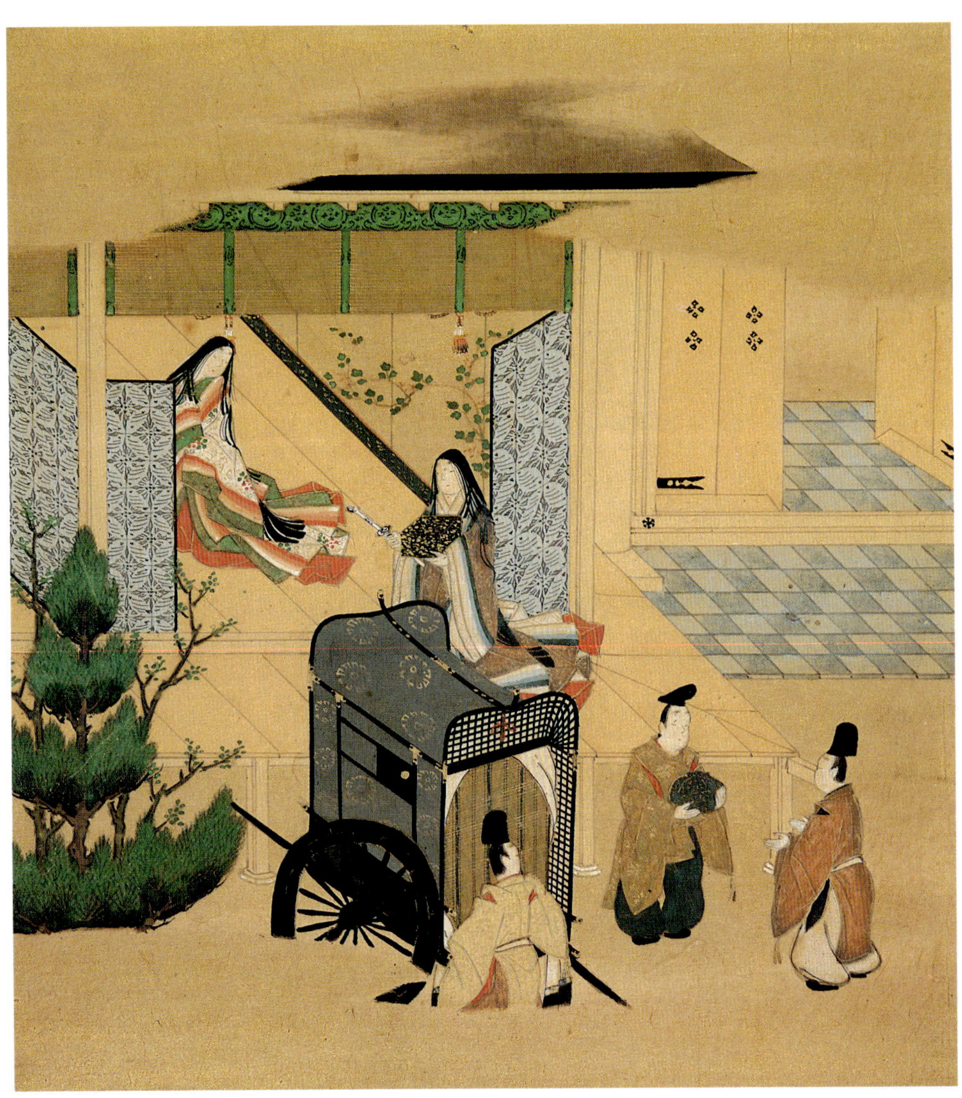

5. Prince Genji promises to look after Princess Akashi (chapter 19, "Usugumo," A Rack of Clouds)

5.

Genji Monogatari Gajō

(The Tale of Genji)

Anonymous

Middle of 17th century, Edo period

One album; ink, colors, silver, and gold on paper

H 23.5 W 21.5

CBJ No. 1041 (62)

Six *Tosa-e*-style paintings in rich coloring are accompanied by either a poem or a piece of prose according to each subject. The ladies' facial expressions in particular are somewhat similar to those depicted by Tawaraya Sōtatsu (?–1643), a Rimpa painter and son of a wealthy merchant, whose studio made fans and pictures for placement on folding screens. He was the first artist from the merchant class to achieve the distinctive title of *hokkyō*.[4]

The paper used for the texts is an elegant quality of *shikishi,* with grass and landscape designs applied with gold ink.

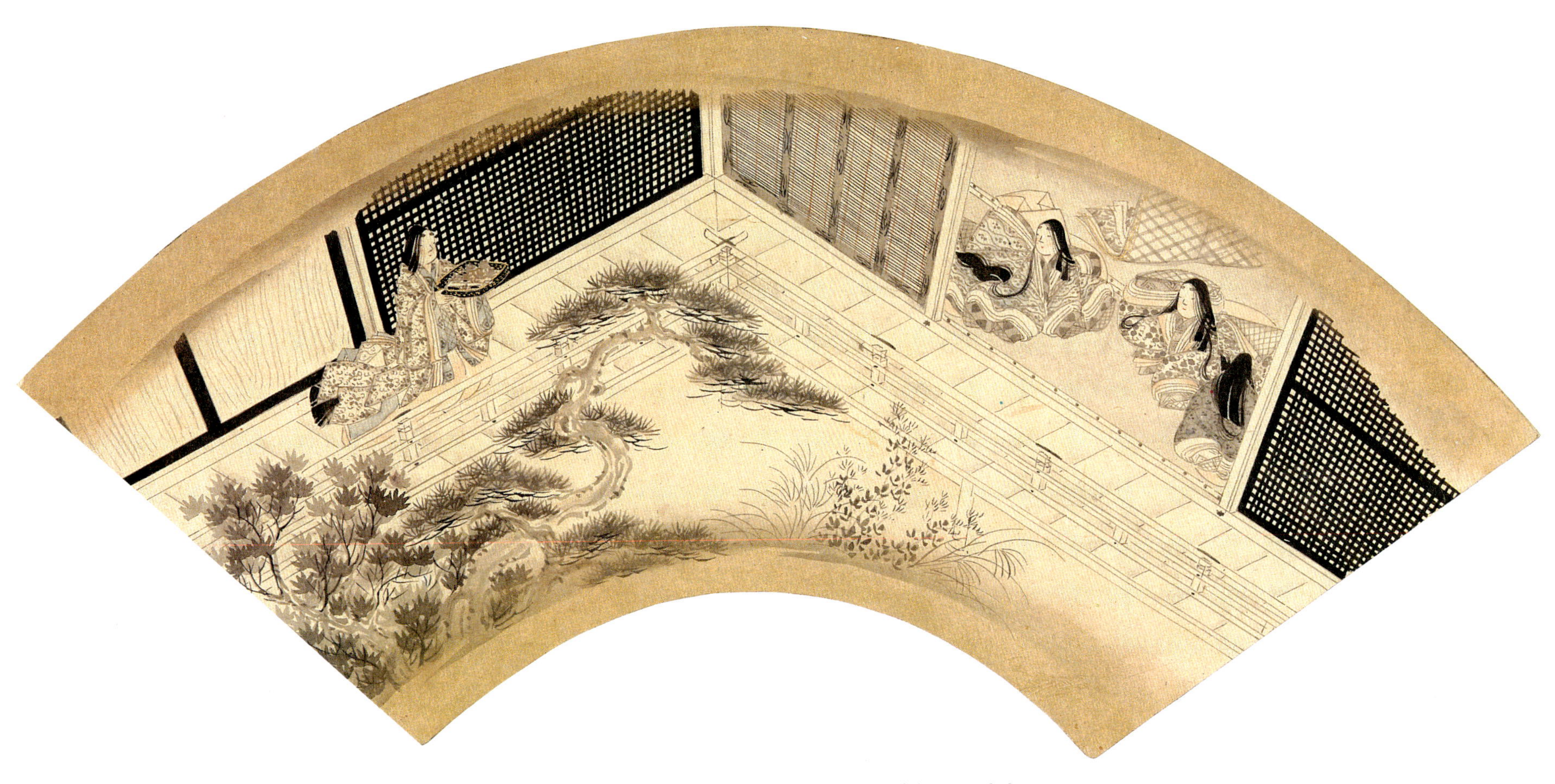

6. A maiden brings a gift to Murasaki from the Akikonomu lady (chapter 21, "Otome," The Maiden)

6.

Genji Monogatari Utaejō

(Poems and paintings album of *The Tale of Genji*)

Anonymous

End of 17th century, Edo period

One album; ink, light colors, and gold on paper

H 39.2 W 28.8

CBJ No. 1002 (51)

The concertina-style album contains fifty-four paintings, mostly on fan-shape paper and some on decorative square paper called *shikishi.* The paintings are all in a refined grisaille style *(hakubyō-e)* with faint touches of light blue. Although they are rather small, the artistic style lends the works a highly dignified air, and they somewhat resemble Sumiyoshi Jokei's style of Genji paintings in the Hakutsuru Museum of Art in Japan.[5]

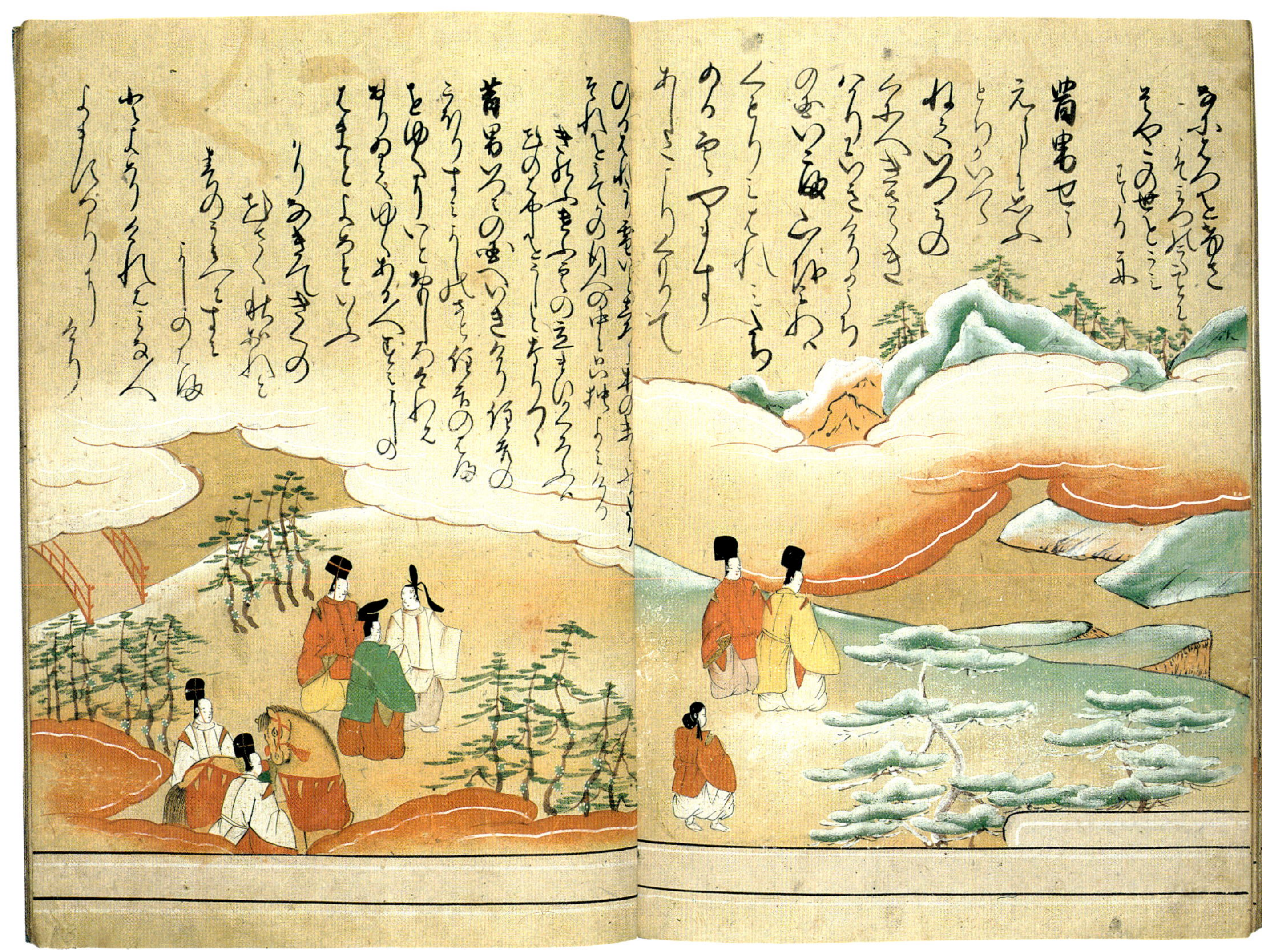

7. Admiring scenery at the beach of Sumiyoshi

7.

Ise Monogatari
(The Tale of Ise)
Anonymous
Middle of 16th century, Momoyama period
Three volumes; ink, colors, silver, and gold on paper
H 29.8 W 22.3 (each)
CBJ No. 1050 (2)

The mid-tenth century literary classic *The Tale of Ise* is a great example of *uta-monogatari* (tales and poems), a genre of the Heian period (794–1185). *The Tale of Ise,* whose author is unknown, includes 209 *waka* (thirty-one syllable verse) linked by brief passages of narrative prose. According to Professor Murase Miyeko , *uta-monogatari* evolved from the custom of attaching fictional or historical headnotes to *waka* poetry, and the *Ise Monogatari* is the earliest known example of this type of work.[6] Most of the poems are based on the activities and gallant pursuits of the Heian courtier/poet Arihara no Narihira (825–880). The theory that he was the author of this thrilling adventury story is no longer accepted, but to some extent the collection gives the impression of being a quasi-biographical account of this famous poet due to its emphasis on his romantic exploits.

Ideal in length and theme, *Ise Monogatari* was a very popular subject for illustrated narratives, yet not many contemporary copies are extant. The Chester Beatty work, one of the finest examples of *Ise Monogatari* from the Momoyama period (1573–1603), contains all 125 chapters, which include 209 poems, and are chronologically arranged. The paintings are of the finest early *nara-ehon* style, in bright colors, particularly vivid orange and green, with plenty of gold leaf. The manner of painting is somewhat simplistic yet possesses a certain lyrical quality and beauty. Of particular interest are the texts written on the stylized clouds above the illustrations. The integration of text with image is considered to be a development of the style of narrative painting in the Muromachi (1333–1573) as well as the early Edo period.

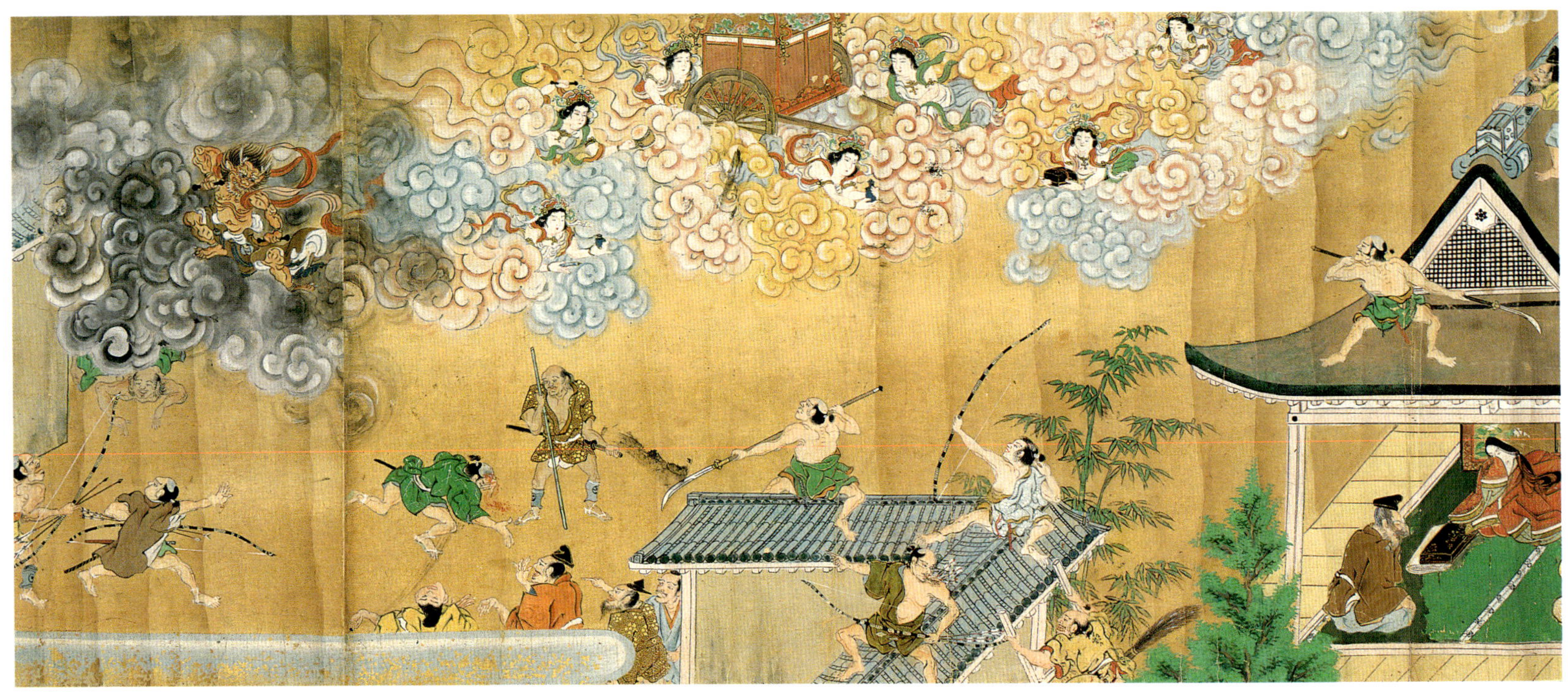

8. Trying to prevent the Shining Princess' return to the Palace of the Moon

8.

Taketori Monogatari
(The Tale of the Bamboo Cutter)
Anonymous
Beginning of 17th century, Edo period
Two scrolls; ink, colors, silver, and gold on paper
I: H 27.5 L 1523; II: H 27.5 L 1365
CBJ No. 1125 (3)

The original story is said to be the oldest novel in Japanese literature. An illusion to it is made in *The Tale of Genji,* so it would seem to have been written between 850 and 950. Although it is called *The Story of Kaguyahime*–"The Shining Princess" in *The Tale of Genji* (chapter 15, "Yomogiu," The Wormwood Patch), there are no copies of the tale under the title *Kaguyahime.* Rather they appear under the title *Taketori Monogatari.*

This romantic fairy tale centers around an old bamboo cutter, a shining princess, and her five suitors. One day when the old bamboo cutter is working, he finds a child of supernatural beauty in the stem of a bamboo tree. He then rears her as his daughter, calling her Shining Princess on account of her brilliant beauty. Miraculously, he becomes a rich man and urges the Shining Princess to marry one of five noble suitors. She in turn sends each of them on a strange quest. Each suitor either fails to perform his task or pretends to have completed it only to have his trickery discovered. The Shining Princess even refuses the attentions of the emperor. Finally she explains to her parents that she comes from the Palace of the Moon, from where messengers are coming to take her back. All efforts to prevent their arrival are fruitless. Putting on a robe of white feathers whose magic powers erase all memories of the earthly world, the Shining Princess departs, leaving behind a letter and an elixir of life for the emperor. Not wishing to prolong his life without her, the emperor has both burned on the top of Mount Fuji, the nearest point to heaven.

The paintings are of a comparatively early *nara-ehon* style, and the final section portraying the departure of the Shining Princess to heaven is of exceptionally lavish execution.

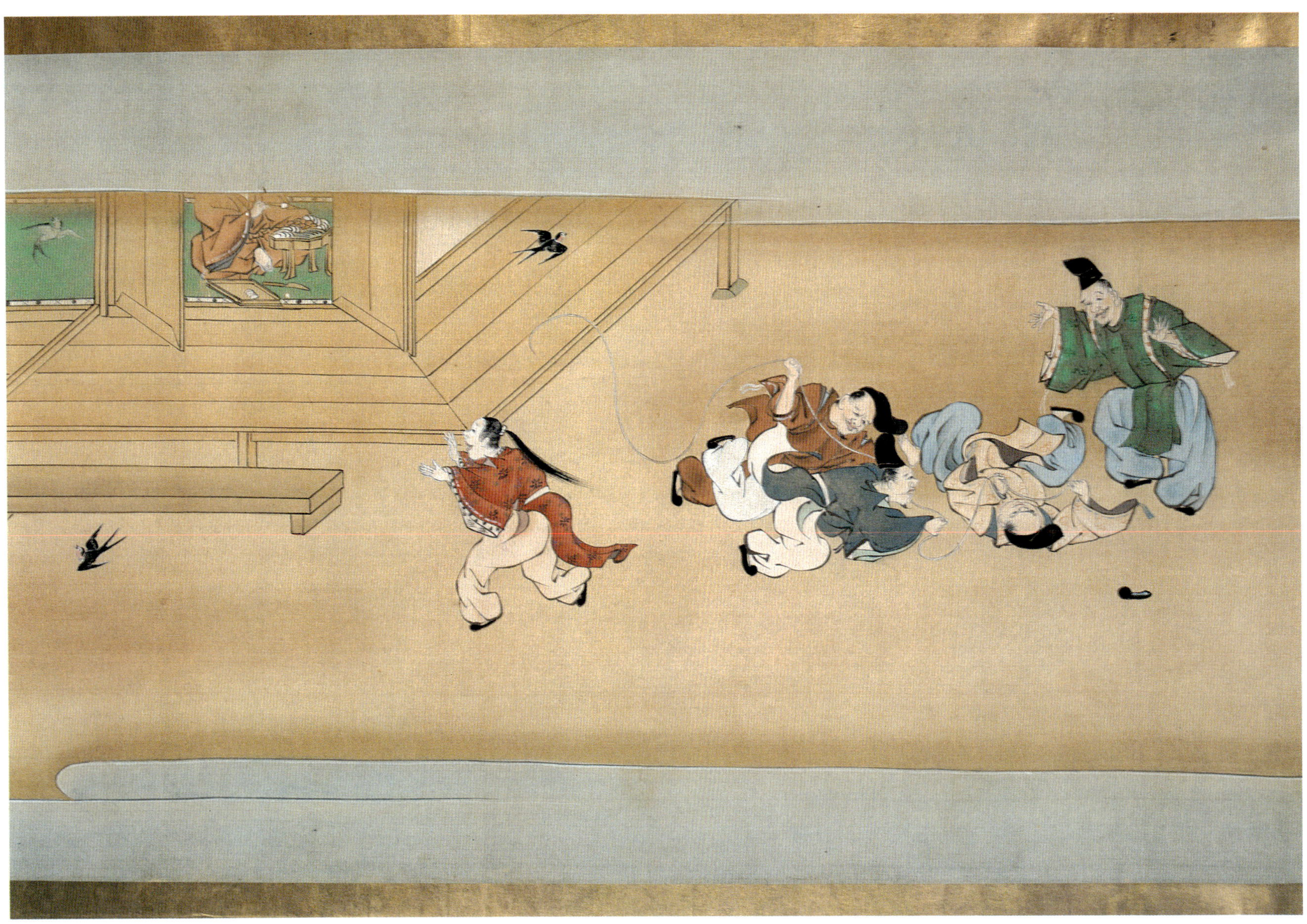

9. Discovering that one of the Shining Princess' suitors failed his quest

9.

Taketori Monogatari Emaki

(The Tale of the Bamboo Cutter)

Itaya Hironaga, painter (1761–1814); Toyama Mitsuhiro, calligrapher (dates unknown)

Beginning of 19th century, Edo period

Three scrolls; ink, colors, and gold on silk

I: H 41 L 332; II: H 41 L 349; III: H 41 L 290

CBJ No. 1163 (73)

Each of the three short scrolls contains only one scene followed by a related text. The scenes depict three of the Shining Princess' suitors, all of whom failed to accomplish their designated tasks (see cat. no. 8).

The illustrations were elegantly painted by Itaya Hironaga, an artist of the Sumiyoshi school. The paintings as well as the calligraphy by Toyama Mitsuhiro on these silk scrolls are of sophisticated and gracious quality.

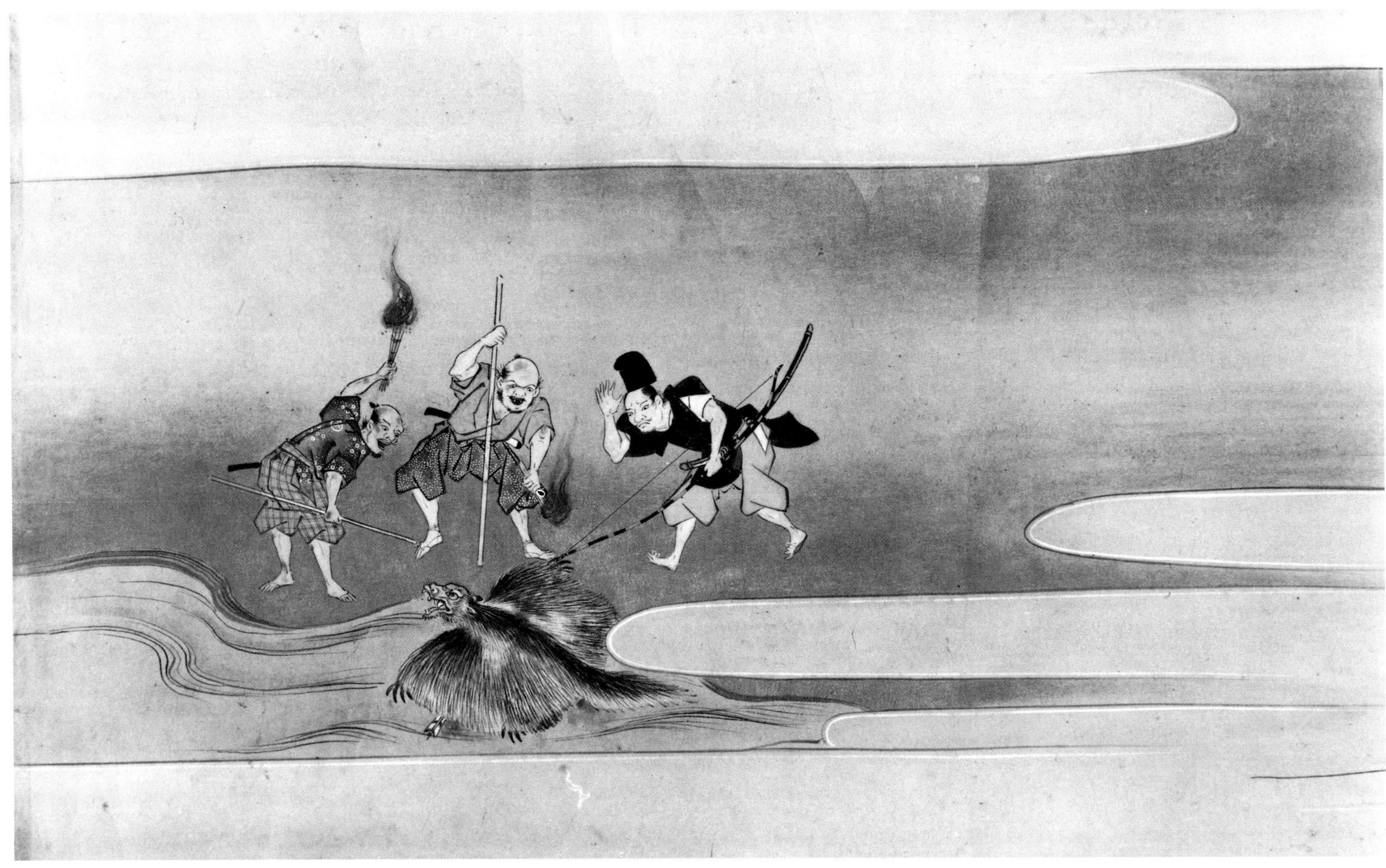

10. An archer shoots a giant flying squirrel

10.

Uji Shūi Monogatari Emaki

(Painted scroll of *The Tales of Uji Shūi*)

Anonymous

Beginning of 18th century, Edo period

One scroll; ink, colors, silver, and gold on paper

H 30 L 2058

CBJ No. 1113 (72)

The Tales of Uji Shūi is an anonymous collection of 197 short stories drawn from Buddhism and Japanese folklore. Its topics range broadly from edifying accounts of miracles worked by Kannon, the goddess of mercy, and of rebirth in the western paradise of Amida, to tales of the supernatural, such as that of the coffin which stubbornly refused to stay buried and returned to the home of its occupant. Folktales, such as the legend of the grateful sparrow or the old man who had a wen on his face that was removed by demons, and humorous or sometimes grotesque incidents drawn from the everyday life of the people are featured as well. The collection constitutes an invaluable document of ideas and beliefs commonly held in Japan in the thirteenth and fourteenth centuries.

This scroll contains five stories:

1. A priest, Jōkan, offers prayers for rain (chapter 20)
2. At Minase, an expert archer shoots a giant flying squirrel (chapter 159)
3. Eastern people forbid sacrificial offerings (chapter 119)
4. A pirate in Settsu experiences a religious awakening and becomes a priest (chapter 123)
5. Boddhidharma watches a game of Go played by elderly priests (chapter 137)

Although the names of the artist and the calligrapher are not known, the paintings somewhat resemble the famous scroll of the same title by Sumiyoshi Jokei in the Idemitsu Museum of Art in Tokyo. It is likely that the Chester Beatty scroll may have been painted by some followers of Sumiyoshi Jokei.

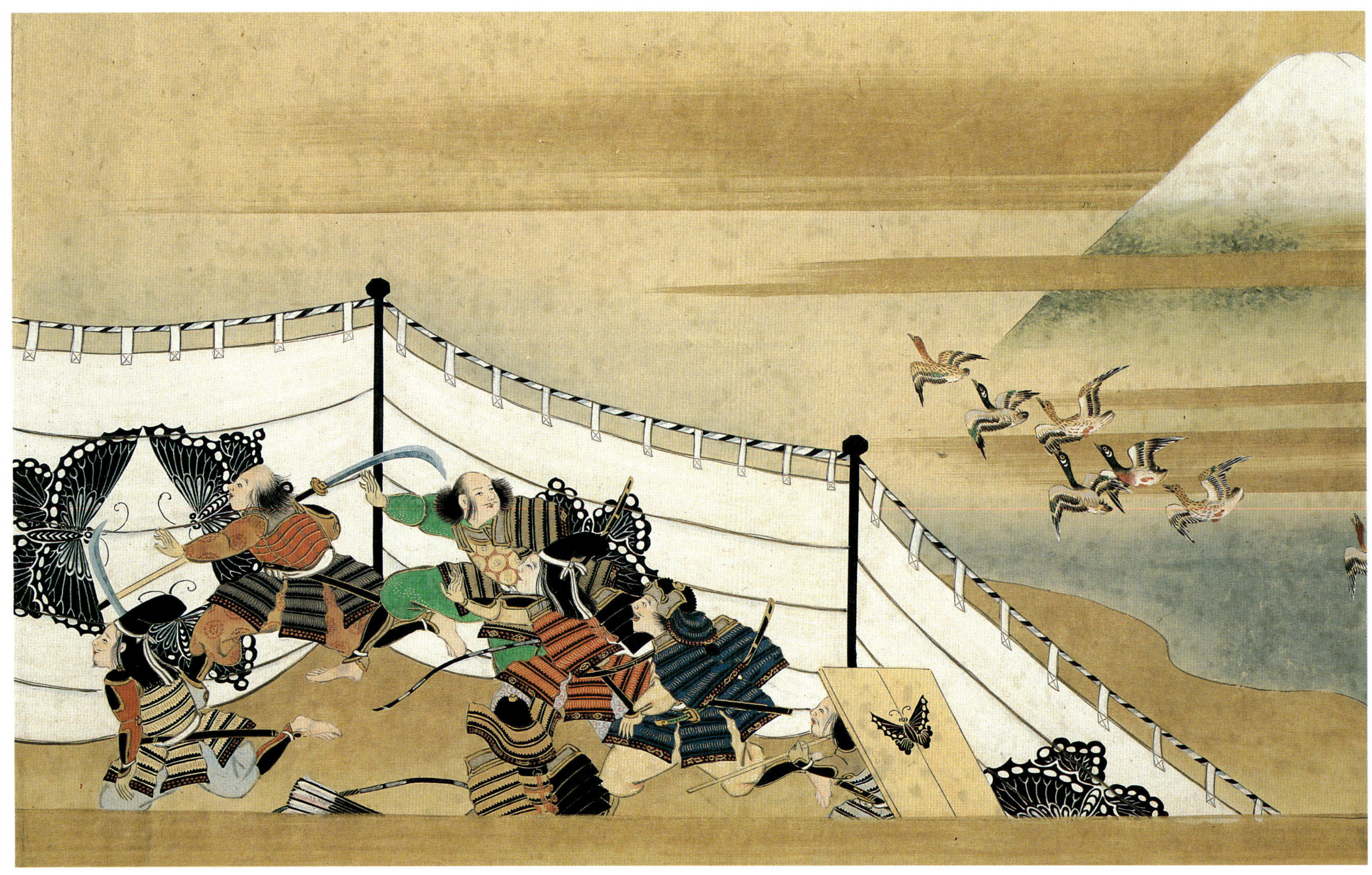

11. Before leaving for battle

11.

Heiji Monogatari Emaki

(The Tale of Heiji)

Anonymous

Middle of 17th century, Edo period

One scroll; ink, colors, silver, and gold on paper

H 31 L 1025

CBJ No. 1148 (21)

This is the final scroll from a set of fifteen. The tale concerns a brief war between the Taira and Minamoto clans that occurred in the winter of the first year of the Heiji era (1160). Titled "Minamoto Yoritomo raises a loyal army and tries to defeat the Taira clan," the scroll depicts the episode in minute detail. Although it portrays only a portion from an entire story, this scroll is a remarkable example of war painting, executed with a strong sense of drama. Its accurate observations of twelfth-century arms and armor make the scroll a valuable source for study of this field.

12.

Musashibō e Engi

(The Tale of Musashibō Benkei)

After Tosa Mitsuhiro, painter (fl. ca. 1430–45);
Imagawa Ryōshun, calligrapher (dates unknown)
Middle of 16th century, Muromachi period
Three scrolls; ink, colors, silver, and gold on paper
I: H 34 L 1387; II: H 34 L 1259;
III: H 34 L 1271
CBJ No. 1117 (1)

As an adored Japanese national hero, Benkei is regarded as the paragon of Japanese patriotism and chivalry. The story of the powerful monk-warrior's life is largely bound up with that of Minamoto Yoshitsune, a famous war lord of the Minamoto clan (ca. 1159–89). These scrolls depict the legendary story of Benkei: the strange birth of this inhuman giant in the mountains, his wild manners, his meeting with Yoshitsune on Gojō Bridge in Kyoto, and the subsequent relationship between the master Yoshitsune and his follower Benkei.

The early popularity of this tale suggests that many painted scrolls and albums must have been produced on the subject. There is, however, no record of other extant copies of painted scrolls of this story.

The paintings indicate a transition in style from *yamato-e* to *nara-e*. Although the black lacquer box containing the scrolls bears the titles and names of the artists Imagawa Ryōshun and Tosa Mitsuhiro of the early fifteenth century, it is doubtful whether they were the actual calligrapher and painter of this work.

The dark blue silk brocade covers of each scroll extend to the inner surface to form a decorative opening edge, patterned in plain gold with designs of lotus flowers on the first scroll, chrysanthemum and eulalia on the second scroll, and morning glories on the third.

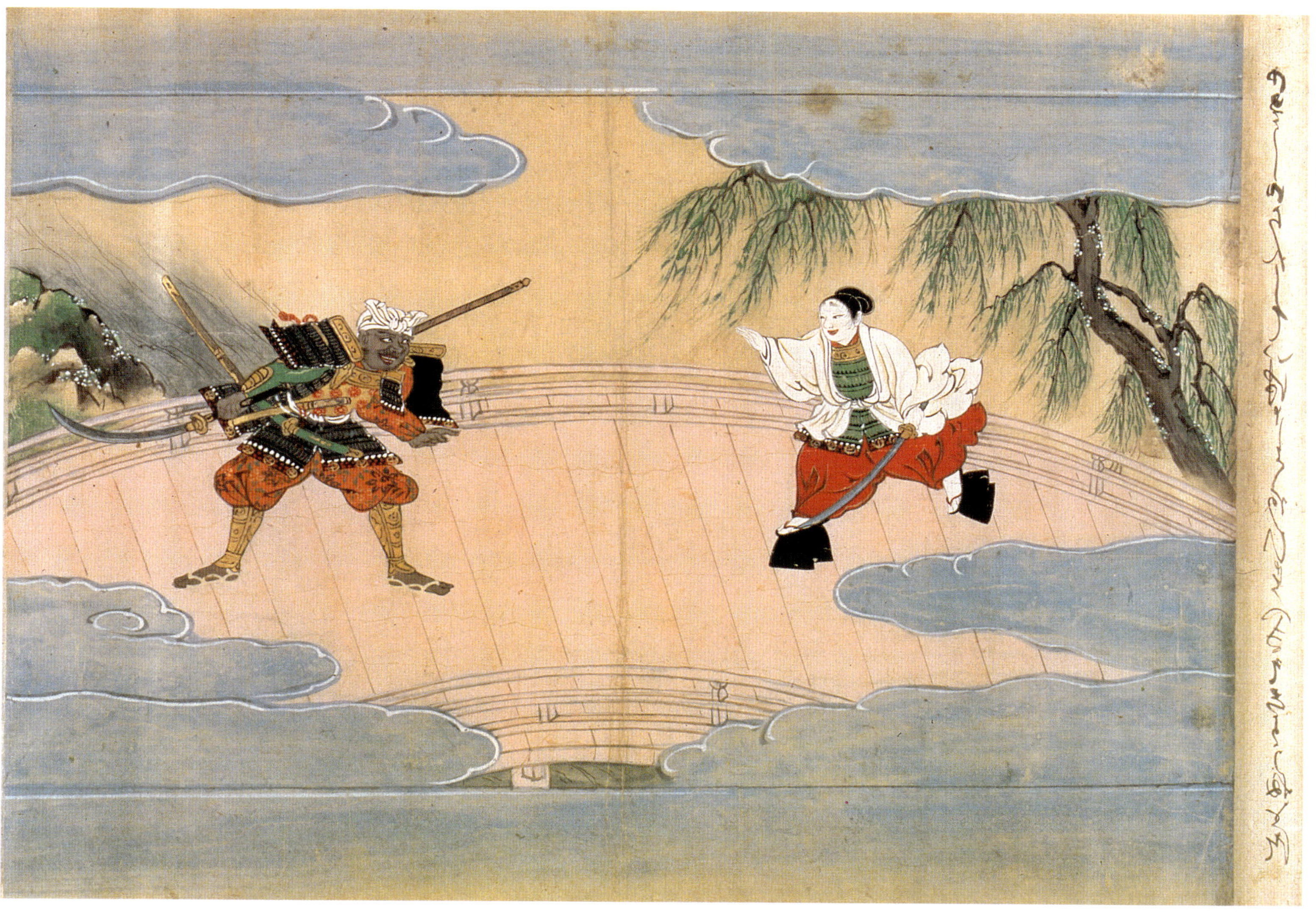

12. Yoshitsune and Benkei fight on Gojō Bridge

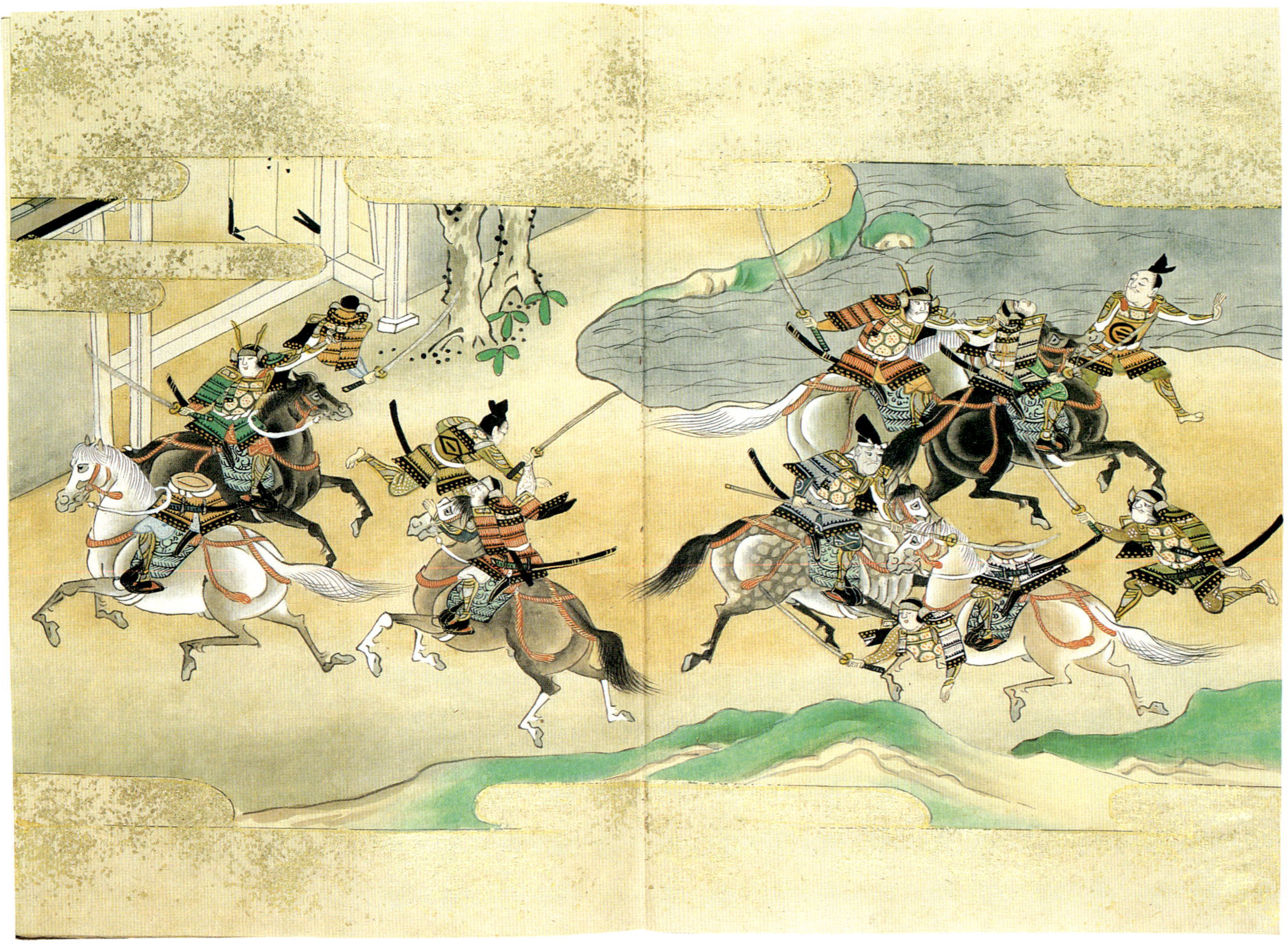

13. Yoshitsune in the midst of combat

13.

Gikeiki

(The Tale of Minamoto Yoshitsune)

Anonymous

Middle of 17th century, Edo period

15 volumes; ink, colors, silver, and gold on paper

H 23.8 W 17 (each)

CBJ No. 1033 (36)

Kōwaka Bukyoku, a kind of theatrical play that was very popular among the samurai (warrior) class during the Muromachi period (1333–1573), was a common subject for *nara-ehon*. In particular, the story of the well-known war lord Minamoto Yoshitsune was one of the most celebrated themes in Kōwaka Bukyoku repertories. Not many copies of this tale still exist, however, and it is likely that the story's length made it unsuitable for frequent treatment in *nara-ehon*. Except for one missing volume (number 12), this is a complete set of the sixteen-volume account of the life of Yoshitsune. In format and style, this set is standard *nara-ehon*.

This version of the Yoshitsune epic tends to recount the more legendary side of the hero rather than his warrior exploits. Childhood experiences (when he was known as Ushiwakamaru) and the strange evil fate that befell him in his latter years are fully described. It is probably because his heroic life is well described in *The Tale of the Taira Clan* and *The Rise and Fall of the Minamoto and the Taira Clan* that it is omitted in this version, while the more humane and noble qualities of Yoshitsune instead receive emphasis. The emotionally moving story vividly depicts the nobility and pathos of this legendary character.

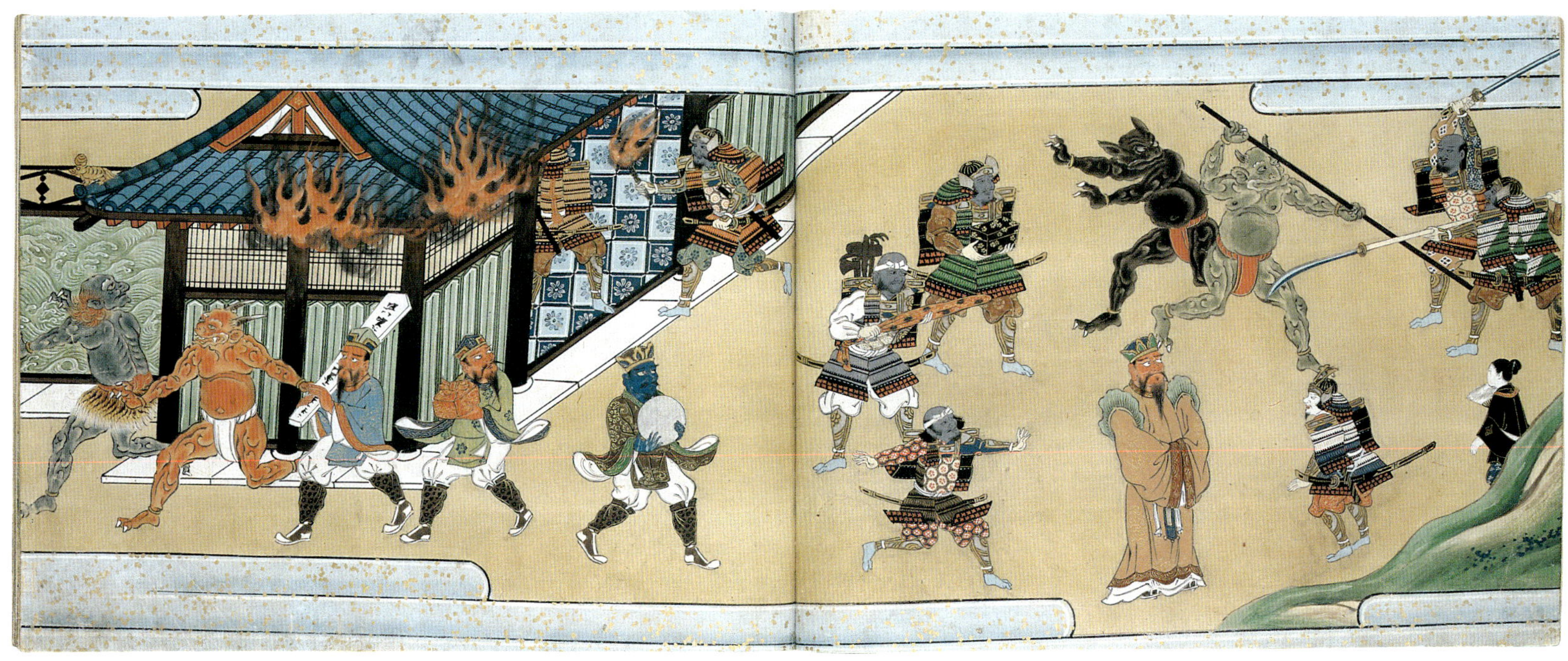

14. Yoshitsune meets Emma at the gate of Hell

14.

Yoshitsune Jigokuyaburi

(The Story of Yoshitsune's Invasion of Hell)

Anonymous

Middle of 17th century, Edo period

Two volumes; ink, colors, and gold on paper

H 24.6 W 32.5 (each)

CBJ No. 1017 (11)

The title seems to be taken from the similar story of "Jōruri," a type of musical narrative or ballad drama. Unusual for *nara-ehon* are the albums' format and covers of yellow silk with painted designs of butterflies on the front and grasses on the back.

The story of Yoshitsune's exploits starts with an encounter between an ascetic and a fierce-looking itinerant priest at the foot of Mount Fuji on the thirteenth day of July. The ascetic is taken to see Hell, where an event is unfolding even though it is a Buddhist feast day during the Bon Festival. Having crossed the River Sanzu, Yoshitsune and his followers invade Hell in an attempt to occupy it. They eventually destroy all its evils, and Yoshitsune becomes its deputy governor. He gradually grows uneasy, however, and becomes a believer in Amida, the lord of the western paradise. Since Yoshitsune is striving to reach paradise, the itinerant mountain priest appears again as a witness to the invasion of Hell, and he preaches the Buddhist teaching of Hell and its evils. As soon as he finishes, the priest disappears into the clouds, at which point Yoshitsune awakens from his dream.

According to Professor Asahara Yoshiko, this caricatured vision of Hell is indicative of people's general conception of it during the Edo period.[7] One detail of particular interest is the small figure of the ascetic portrayed as an onlooker in each illustration.

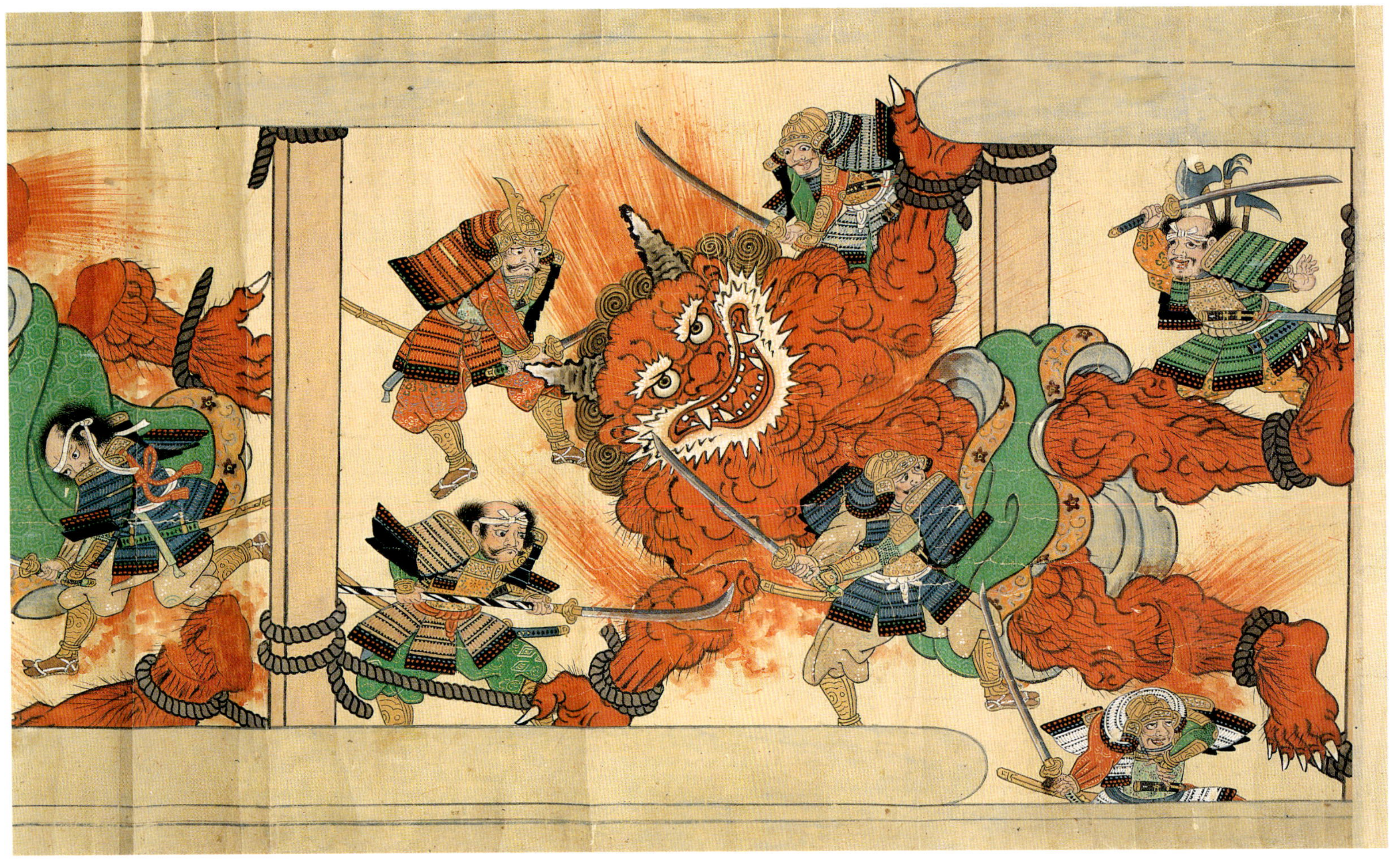

15. Shuten Dōji

15.

Ōeyama Emaki

(The Tale of Ōeyama)

Anonymous

Middle of 17th century, Edo period

Three scrolls; ink, colors, and gold on paper

I: H 33 L 1475; II: H 33 L 1340;

III: H 33 L 1038

CBJ No. 1145 (6)

One of the most well-known heroic stories from medieval Japan is delineated in this set of three scrolls. It tells of the famous episode when Minamoto no Yorimitsu (948–1021), commonly known as Raikō, took the life of the demon Shuten Dōji, who lived at Ōeyama in the Tamba region of Kyoto. The giant demon Shuten Dōji (literally, drunken boy) is described as an ogre, a kidnapper of pretty maidens, and a hairy cannibal disguised as a giant human being.

Hoping for victory in slaying the demon, Raikō and his five fellow comrades (Usui Sadamitsu, Ueda Suetaka, Watanabe no Tsuna, Sakata no Kintoki, and Fujiwara Yasumasa) visit three Shintō shrines to receive the blessing of the deities. Before they leave, the deities present them with two gifts: some wine and a magic golden cap. Following the directions given to them by the deities, Raikō and his men reach the gaudy palace of the ogre. There they are welcomed with a banquet of human flesh and blood. In return, Raikō and his men chop off the ogre's head. A loud clap of thunder is suddenly heard. The giant's head leaps high into the air and lands on Raikō, but the magic cap saves him from harm. The story ends happily with the release of all the beautiful maidens who have been kidnapped, and peace is at last restored to life in Kyoto.

The paintings are executed in a rather rough style with bright colors, while the realism of the horrific scenes of the banquet and the bloody fighting verges on the grotesque.

This tale was one of the most renowned accounts of warriors and their adventures. So popular was the story that another version, set at Ibukiyama in the province of Ōmi (present-day Shiga prefecture), soon circulated.[8] Subsequently called "Ibukiyama Shuten Dōji," it dealt with the life of the giant ogre. Although the Chester Beatty set of scrolls is based on the story of the ogre at Ōeyama, the text is rather similar to the Ibukiyama version and thus provides interesting comparative material for research into the two versions.

16.

Asahina Monogatari

(The Tale of Asahina)

Attributed to Tosa Mitsunobu (1434–1525)

Middle of 17th century, Edo period

One scroll; ink, colors, and gold on paper

H 31.2 L 880

CBJ No. 1132 (56)

A rare medieval short story about a strong man called Asahina is illustrated on this scroll. On the way from the temple where he had been praying for his challenge with the ogres of Hell, Asahina becomes extremely drunk with sake and falls fast asleep. Suddenly a small ogre appears in front of him and taunts him. Chasing after him, Asahina reaches Hell, where he forces Emma, the governor of Hell, to surrender. In return for sparing Emma's life, Asahina is rewarded with all sorts of delicacies. As he is enjoying the entertainment, the mocking words sung by the small ogre reach his ears again. Asahina tries to stand up but stumbles to the ground. At that moment he wakes from his dream, suddenly enlightened to the transitory nature of life.

The scroll contains a full text and five illustrations, of which the fifth seems to be earlier than the others and is attributed to Tosa Mitsunobu. The subject resembles *Yoshitsune Jigokuyaburi* (cat. no. 14), with its caricatured portrayal of Hell, which again suggests that the people of the Edo period had little fear of its horrors. Since no other scroll of this story seems to exist, the Chester Beatty scroll is a valuable piece of research material for scholars.

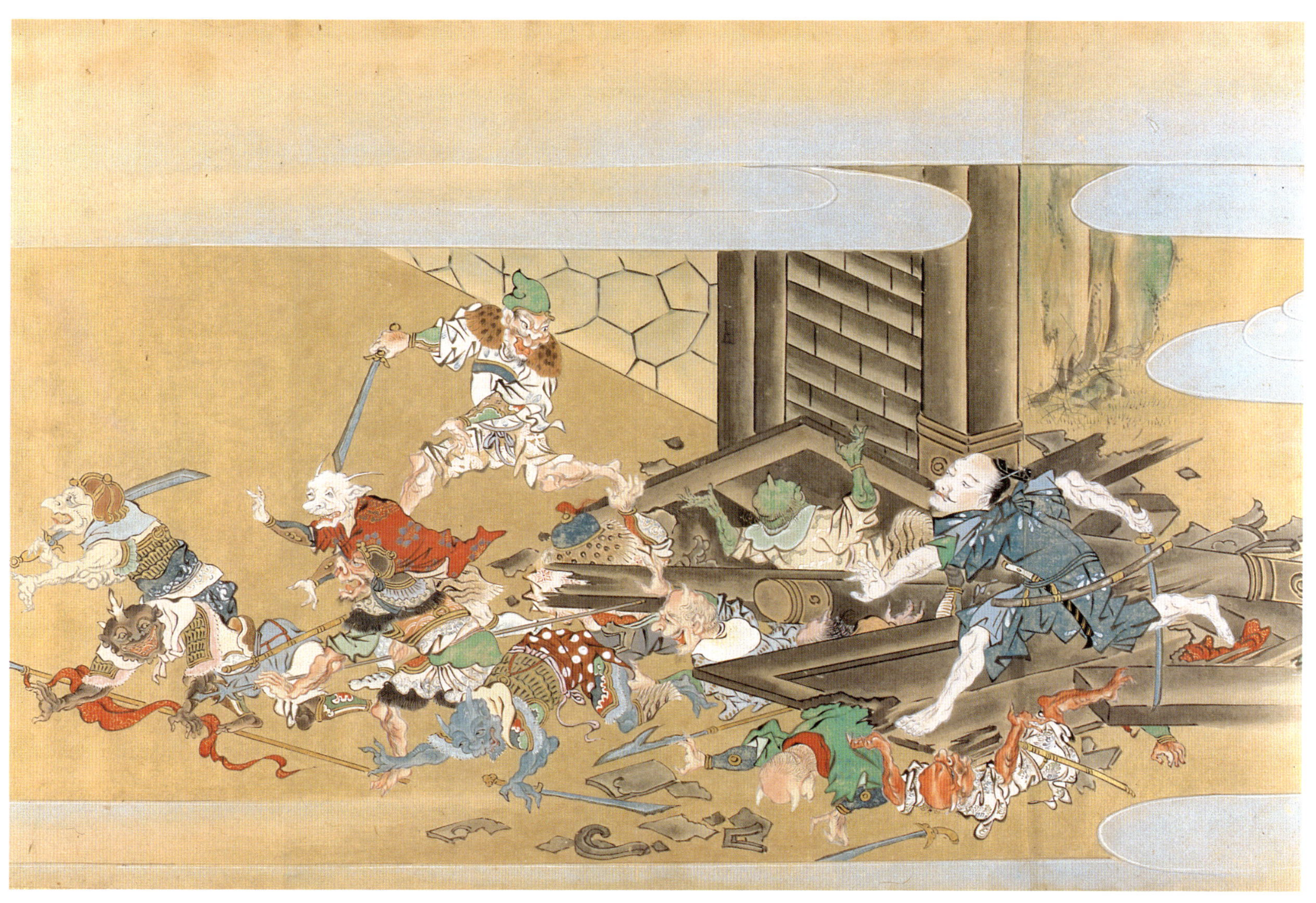

16. Asahina breaks through the gate of Hell

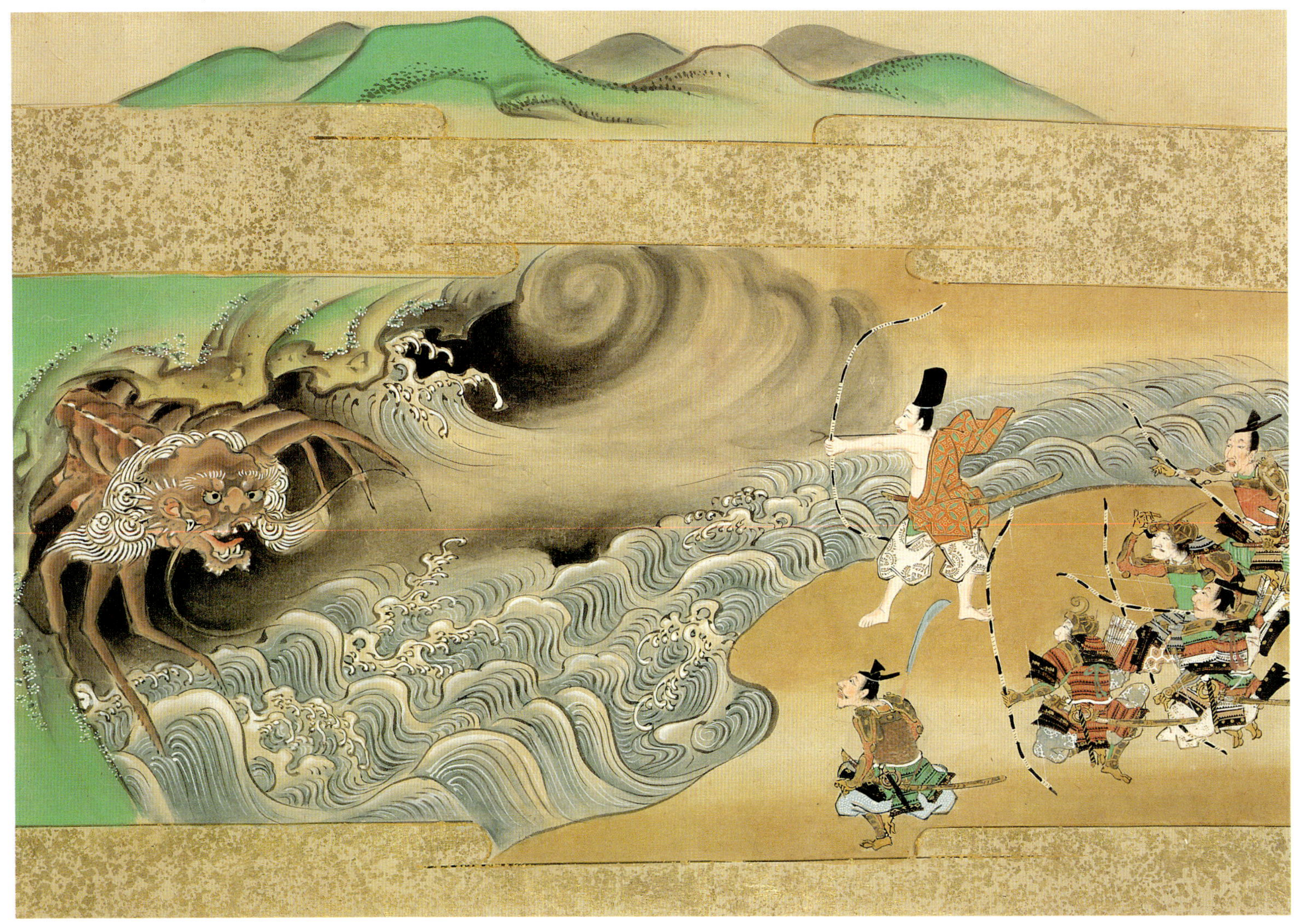

17. Hidesato kills the giant centipede Mukade

17.

Tawara Tōda Emaki

(The Story of Tawara Tōda)

Anonymous

Middle of 17th century, Edo period

Three scrolls; ink, colors, and gold on paper

I: H 33 L 1368; II: H 33 L 1427;

III: H 33 L 1461

CBJ No. 1164 (22)

A famous hero of the tenth century, Fujiwara no Hidesato, commonly referred to as Tawara Tōda, suppressed Taira no Masakado in a civil war. The event for which he is most recognized is the killing of the giant centipede of Mount Mikami, known as Mukade.[9]

One day when Hidesato is about to cross Seta Bridge at Lake Biwa, he is confronted by a great dragon that blocks the narrow path. Undaunted, he steps upon the dragon's head and walks along its back, but he has not gone more than a few steps forward when a dwarfish old man appears and compliments Hidesato on his courage. The old man tells the warrior that he has been waiting for one so brave, and he begs Hidesato to stay and kill the centipede Mukade, which is poisoning the lake and preventing him, the Dragon King, from living in his palace. Hidesato agrees to help, and so the Dragon King, Ryūjin (for the shape of the dwarfish old man was but a disguise), leads the way into the lake.

As midnight approaches, Hidesato sees the huge form of the centipede crawling along, illuminated by lights gleaming from its eyes and its hundreds of legs. As it draws near, Hidesato shoots first one and then a second arrow at the beast's head. With the third arrow, he finally slays the beast. Straightaway all the lights stop gleaming in its eyes and legs, and the dead body of the centipede sinks to the bottom of the lake. Leading Hidesato back to his palace, Ryūjin introduces the hero to his daughter Oto-hime and rewards him for his bravery with many gifts. Among these is a bag of rice, the contents of which can never be exhausted. From this Hidesato derives his nickname Tawara Tōda, or lord of the rice-bag, and his name is always associated with this legendary story.

Both the illustrations and the calligraphy of these three scrolls are of standard *nara-ehon* style.

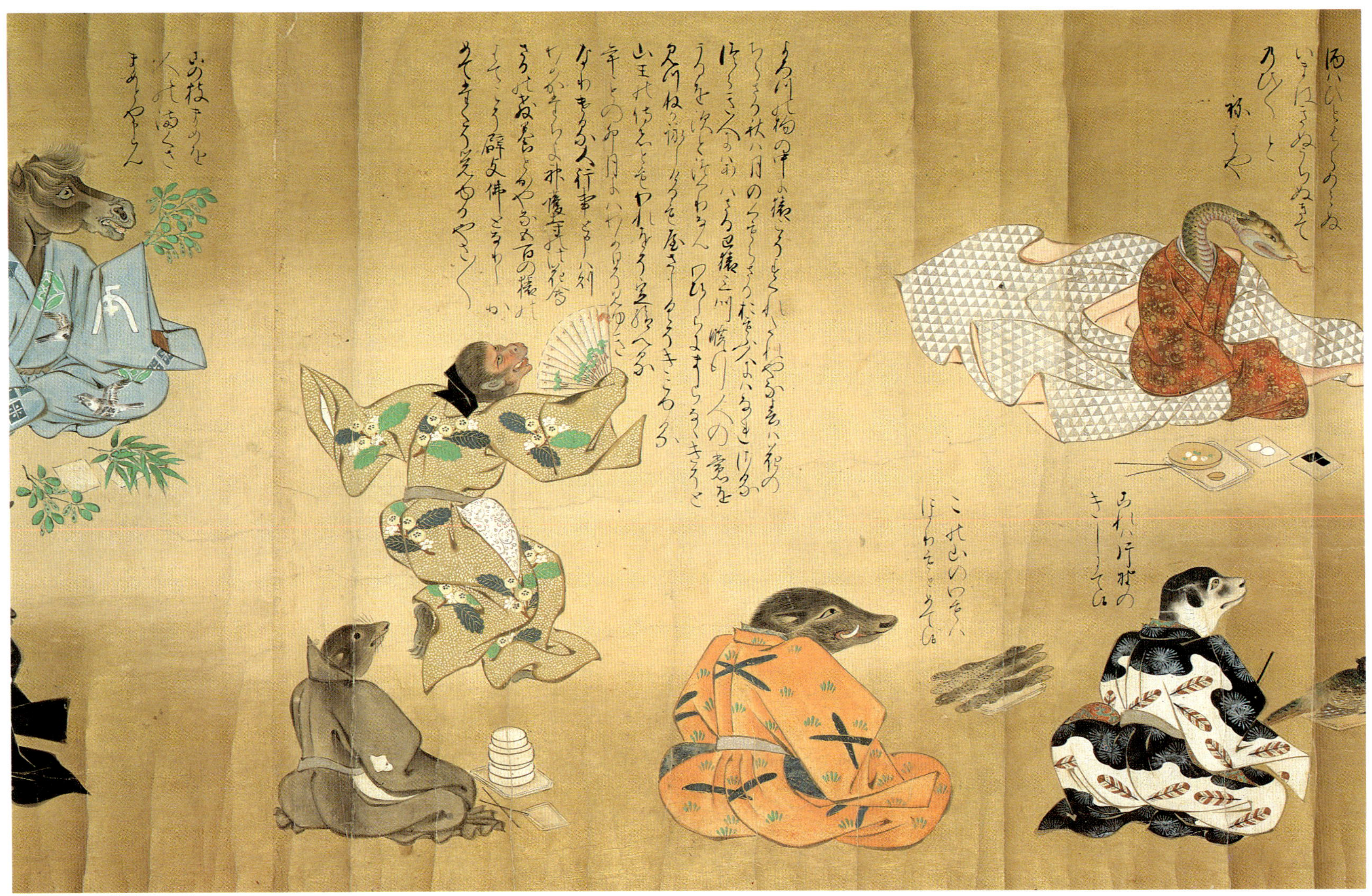

18. Animals in a poetry contest

18.

Jūnirui Utaawase Emaki

(Painted scrolls of a *waka* poetry contest, depicting twelve kinds of beasts and birds)

Anonymous

Middle of 17th century, Edo period

Three scrolls; ink, colors, silver, and gold on paper

I: H 34.5 L 1030; II: H 34.5 L 940;

III: H 34.5 L 1100

CBJ No. 1154 (10)

With the exception of two sections, the Chester Beatty scrolls are similar to a set of well-known scrolls of this subject in the Dōmoto collection in Kyoto. The text of the beginning section, which is missing in the Dōmoto scroll, is identical to the text in the printed book entitled *Kemono Taiheiki,* while two other sections of text recall those found in this book.[10]

The subject is *uta awase*, a *waka* poetry contest that was a popular game among courtiers in the Heian period. Usually poets from the contesting groups of Left and Right were paired against each other. In the first scroll, most of the contestants are seated with their poems beside them. In the second, they prepare for the competition, and in the third the contest is in progress.

The paintings were elegantly executed despite the thick application of bright colors. The subtle designs in gold and silver on the text sections are also of exceptional quality, as are the interesting and amusing words of the competitors, which are described in exquisite calligraphy interspersed among the paintings. These scrolls may have been based on the Dōmoto versions.

19.

Sumiyoshi Monogatari

(The Tale of Sumiyoshi)

Anonymous

Middle of 17th century, Edo period

Three albums; ink, colors, and gold on paper

H 24.6 W 32.3 (each)

CBJ No. 1021 (34)

Designs in ink and the light colors of pine, bamboo, and plum, respectively, indicate the order of the three volumes in this set. The pale yellow silk covers as well as the format of the albums are very unique for *nara-ehon*, while both the paintings and the calligraphy are of standard *nara-ehon* style. Typical is the feature of wide bands of imaginary mists and clouds outlined in black. The format of this set of albums closely resembles that of *Yoshitsune Jigokuyaburi* (cat. no. 14), and they may have been produced in the same studio.

The original story of this title is mentioned in *The Tale of Genji* and in *The Pillow Book* by Sei Shōnagon during the Heian period. *The Tale of Sumiyoshi,* however, is an adapted version written at a much later date (during the Kamakura and Muromachi periods). A young girl, the daughter of a chamberlain called Saemon no Kami, is poorly treated by her stepmother and moves to Sumiyoshi to stay with a nun. Eventually she finds happiness when she meets a courtier who has dreamt of an encounter with this very girl. He welcomes her to Kyoto, where they have a happy life together. This sort of subject was very popular among *nara-ehon* during the Momoyama and Edo periods.

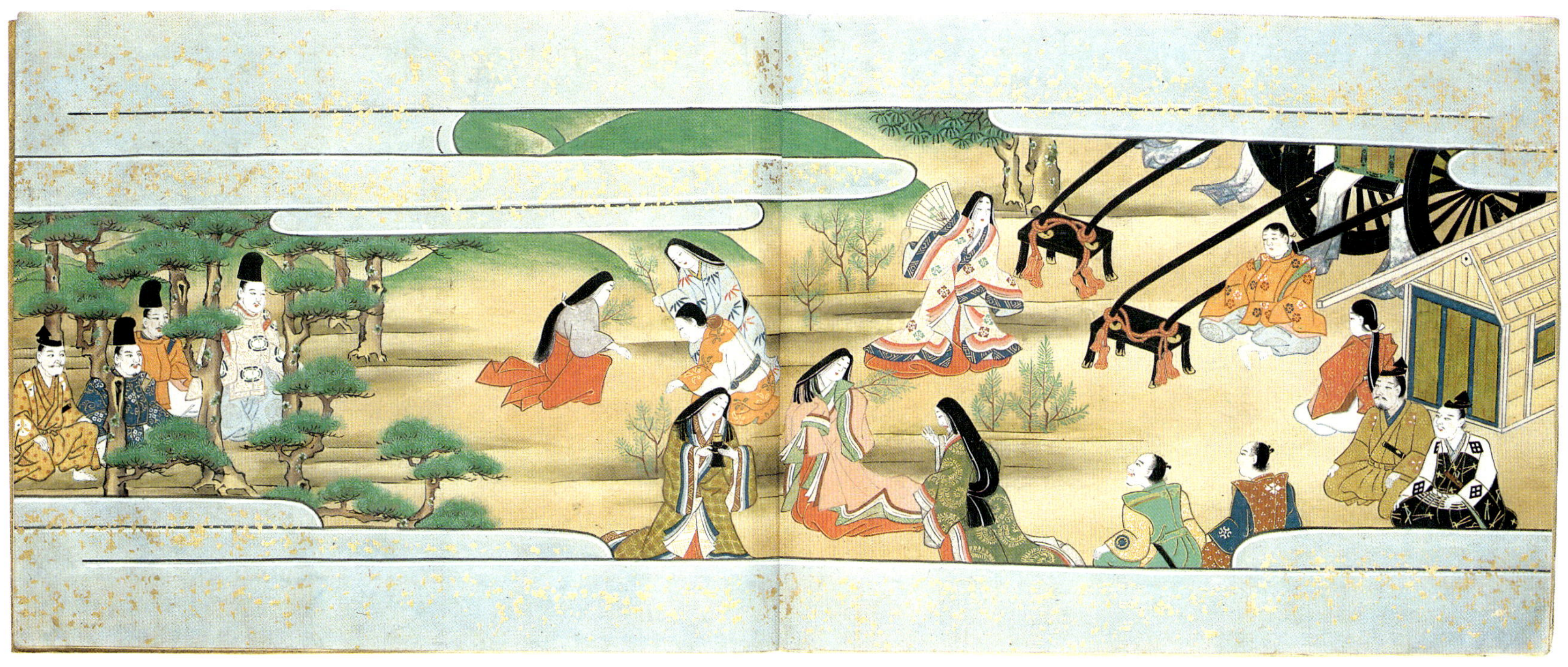

19. Dancing in the garden before courtiers

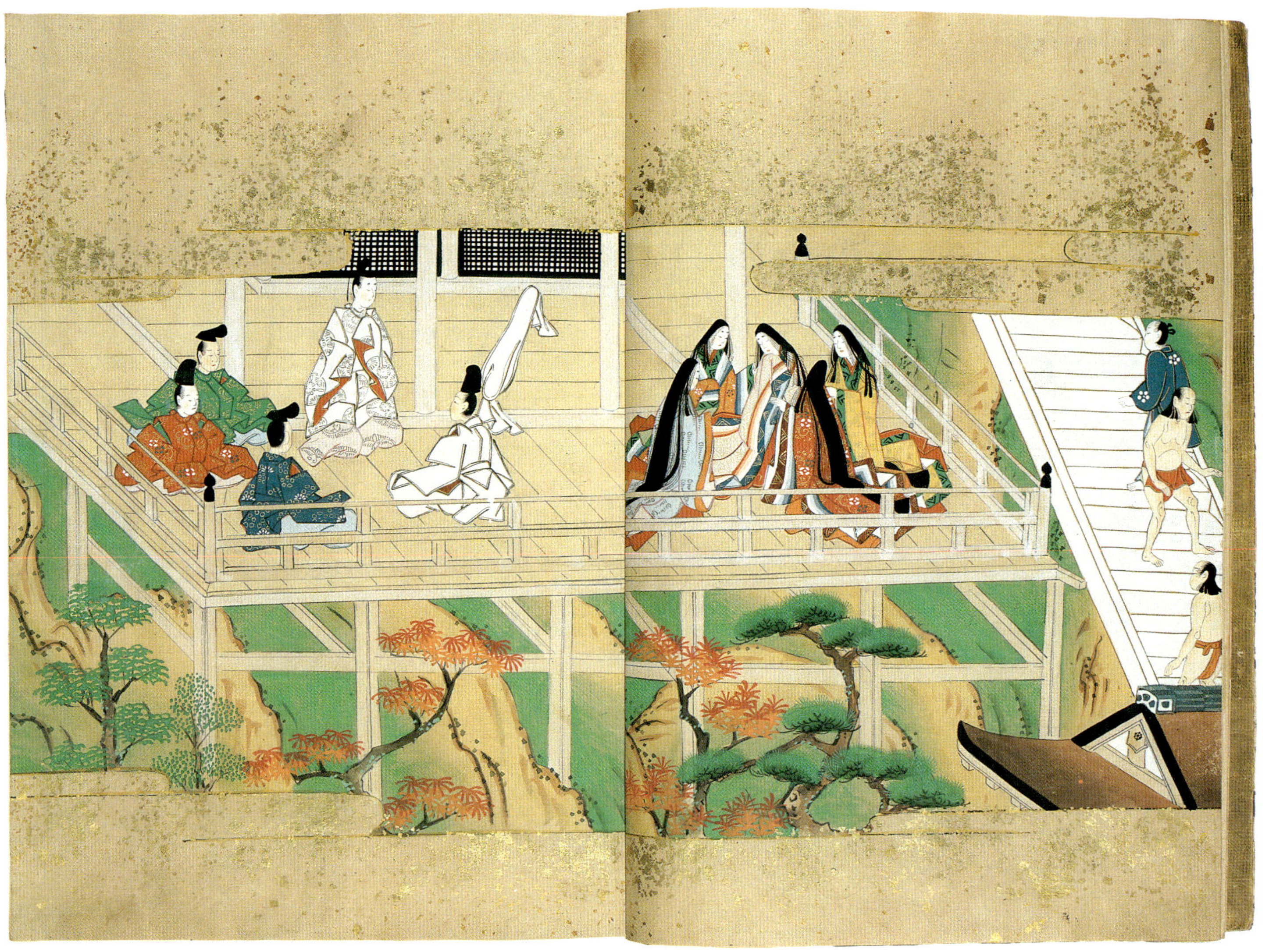

20. Escaping an autumn shower

20.

Shigure (Monogatari)

(An Autumn Shower)

Anonymous

Middle of 17th century, Edo period

Three albums; ink, colors, and gold on paper

H 33 W 44.2 (each)

CBJ No. 1045 (25)

In this story–commonly known as "Shigure," an autumn shower, or "Amayadori," taking shelter from the rain–an ill-fated orphan princess escapes an autumn shower when she visits Kiyomizu Temple in Kyoto. There she meets a young nobleman who has also come there to seek shelter from the rain. Naturally they soon fall in love. The young man's father, however, does not approve of his son's marriage, since he is a man of powerful ambition and desires to see his son wed to the daughter of a highly ranked courtier. Separated from the young nobleman, the sad princess spends a lonely life in the country, when in due course the reigning emperor hears of her. He asks her to marry him and become his empress. Despite the seeming happiness of their marriage, the empress cannot help thinking of the young nobleman for whom she laments. He in turn retires into monastic seclusion, grief-stricken because he can no longer see the princess.

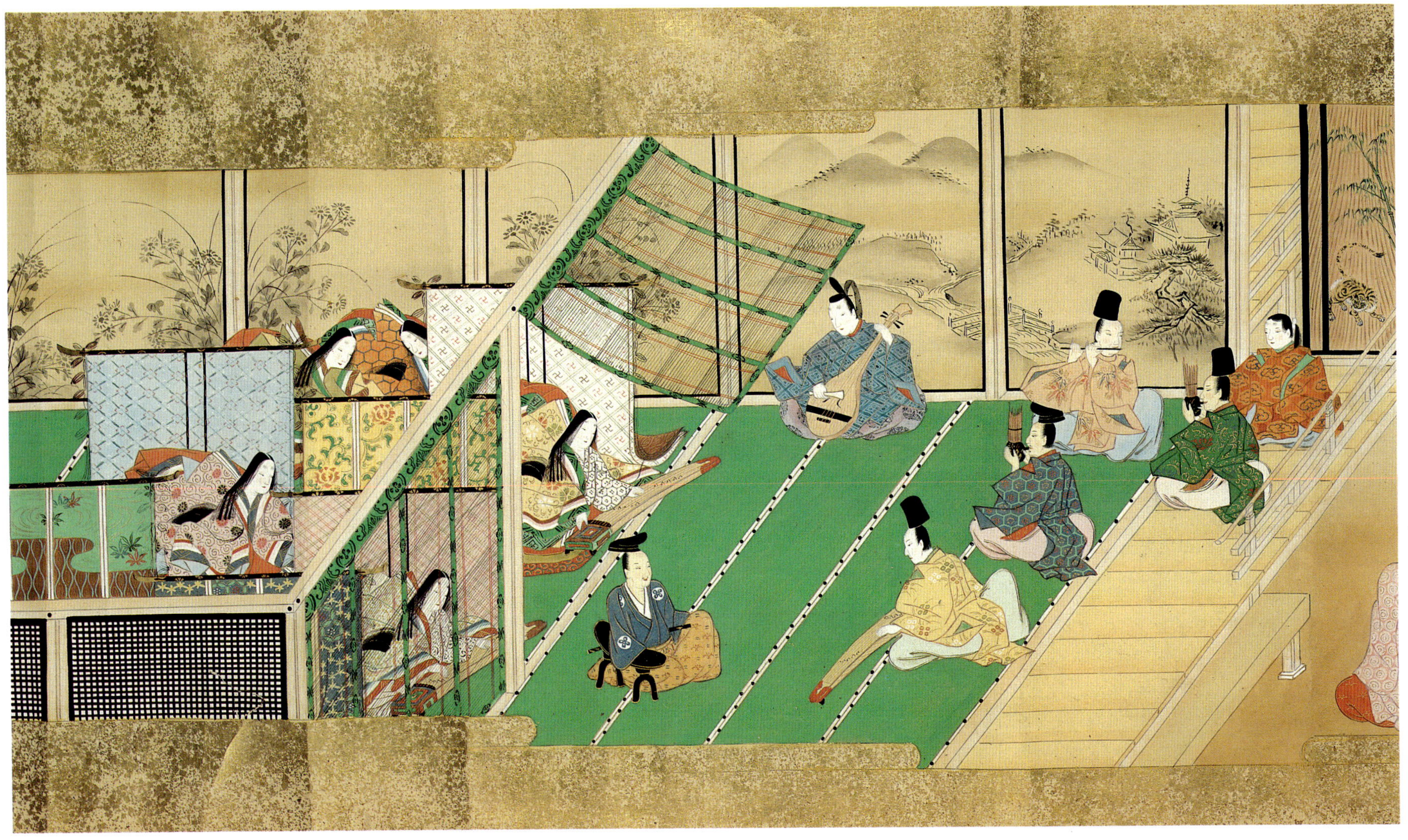

21. Court nobles and Bunshō's daughters play music together

21.

Bunshō no Sōshi Emaki

(The Tale of Bunshō)

Anonymous

Middle of 17th century, Edo period

Two scrolls; ink, colors, silver, and gold on paper

I: H 33 L 1400; II: H 33 L 1415

CBJ No. 1186 (9)

Bunshō is a poor laborer who serves the Shintō deity of Kashima Shrine. The high priest of the shrine, trying to test Bunshō's piety and faith, orders him to leave the sacred place and dedicate himself to his own work. Leaving the shrine, Bunshō goes to work as a salt-maker in Kashima. Helped by his steady devotion to the god of Kashima Shrine, he achieves brilliant success. He and his wife, however, are unhappy because they have no children, and they return to the shrine to pray to the great deity. Soon they are blessed with two beautiful daughters. When they grow up, the girls are successfully married to court nobles from Kyoto. Moreover, Bunshō himself is appointed minister of state and soon afterwards is promoted to senior councilor.[11]

A typical example of *nara-ehon,* with its combination of rich bright colors and highlights of silver and gold, *The Tale of Bunshō* met with great popularity during the Edo period, when Kashima was famous for its salt-making industry. Apart from its importance as an everyday commodity, salt is also of great sacred value in the Shintō religion of Japan. Even today, it is commonly used in purifying rituals, as often seen in sumō wrestling matches. Painted scrolls or albums of this tale served as fashionable gifts for New Year celebrations and often formed part of wedding dowries due to the story's happy ending.

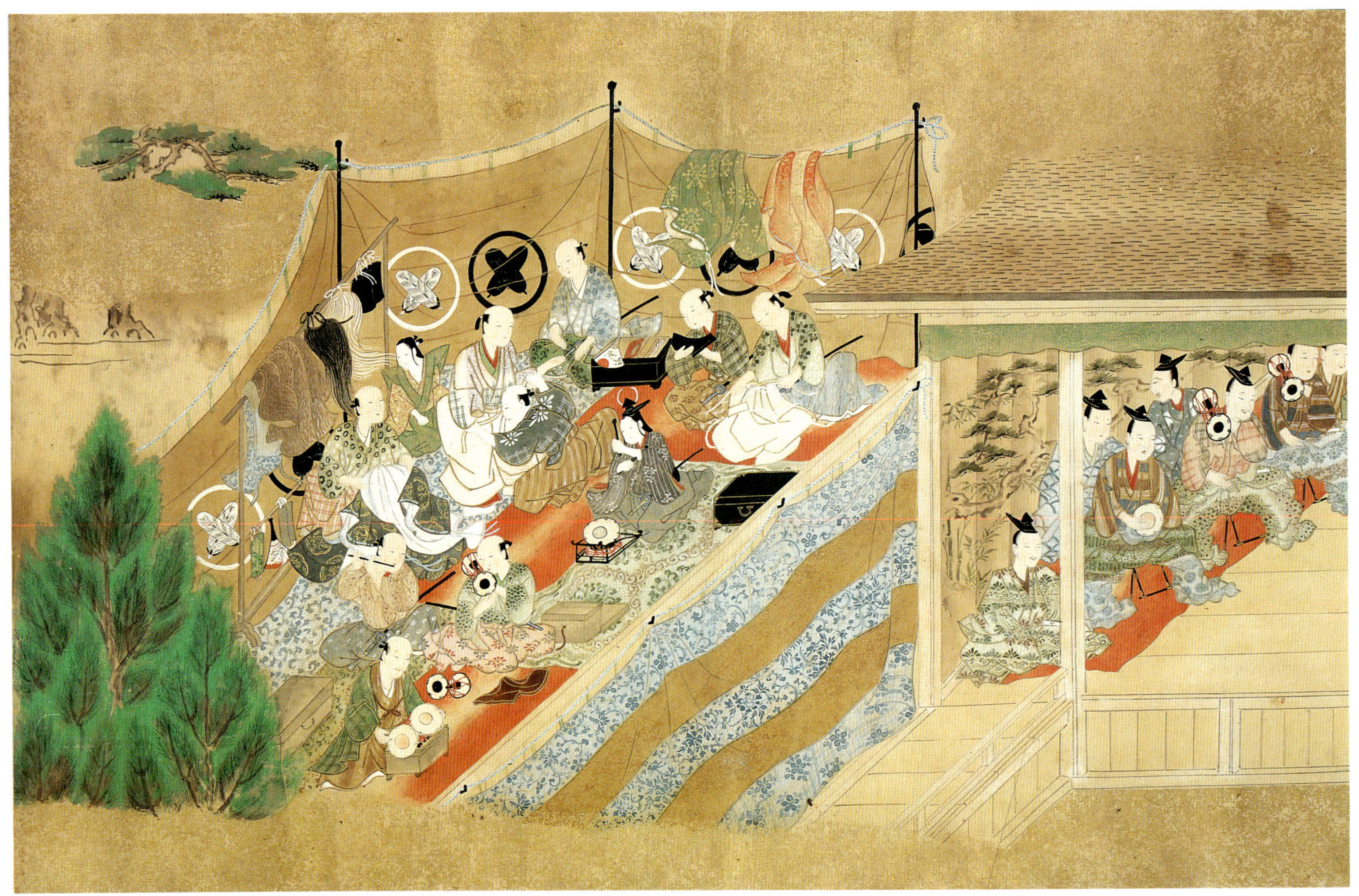

22. An audience watches a Noh performance

22.

Manzai no Tsutsumi Emaki

(Painted scroll of scenes from a Noh play)

Anonymous

Middle of 17th century, Edo period

One scroll; ink, colors, silver, and gold on paper

H 34 L 667

CBJ No. 1111 (15)

No text accompanies these paintings, the first of which appears to be by a different artist and is certainly superior to the others. All the paintings, with their vivid colors and touches of gold, are nevertheless elaborate in execution.

The first scene depicts a performance of the Noh play *Okina* (an old man), traditionally performed at the beginning of a special festive occasion, while the remaining scenes show the several ports of Naniwa (present-day Osaka). One such scene portrays the arrival of a Chinese boat carrying Kureha and Ayaha, two weaver maidens from China. This scroll seems to represent a collection of scenes from Noh plays assembled for a special occasion of celebration known as Shūgen Noh.

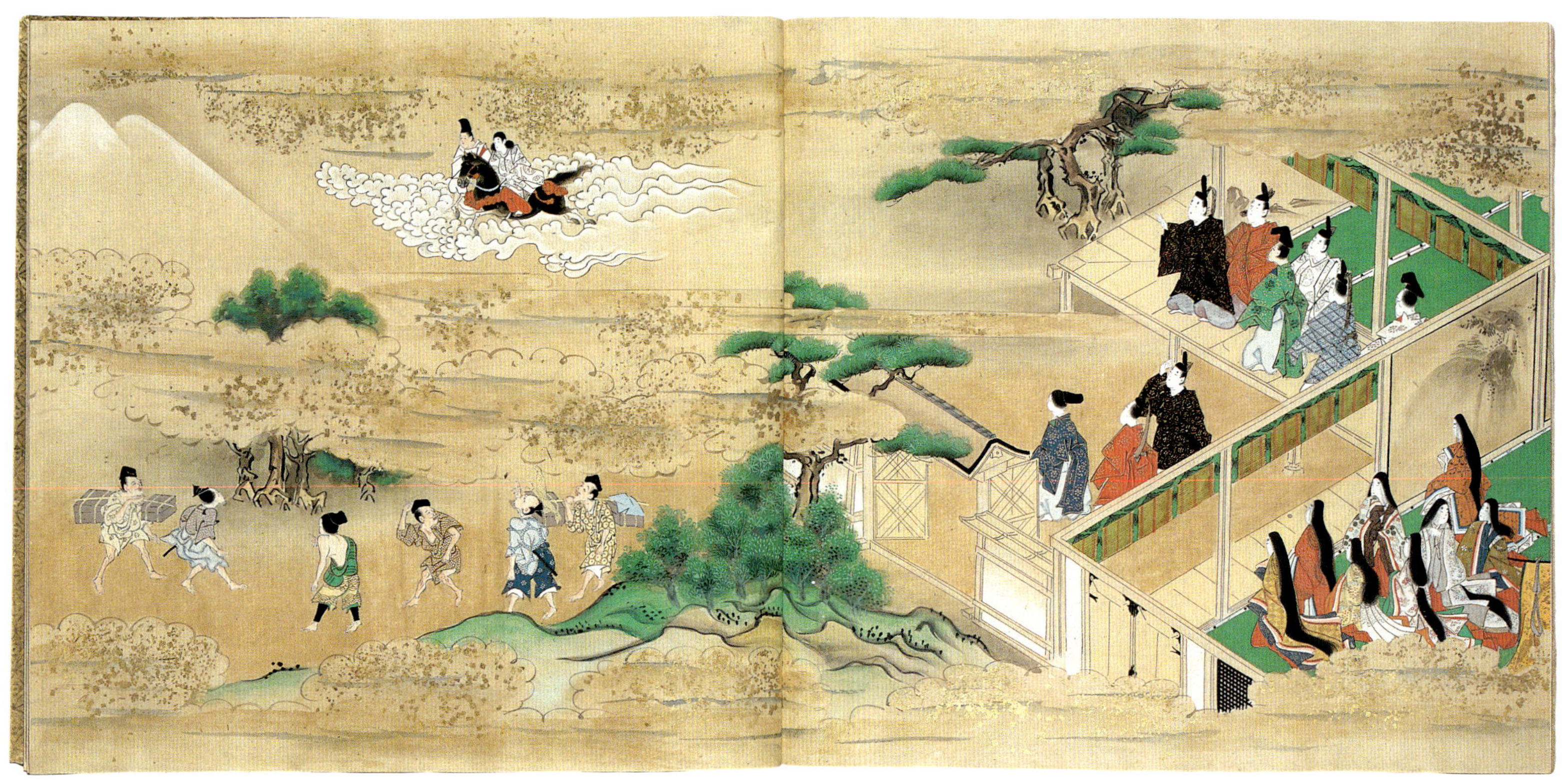

23. Prince Shōtoku tours the country on a horse

23.

Shōtoku Taishi Den

(The Biography of Prince Shōtoku)

Anonymous

Middle of 17th century, Edo period

Five volumes; ink, colors, silver, and gold on paper

H 29.2 W 32.2 (each)

CBJ No. 1004 (19)

Prince Shōtoku (574–622), second son of Emperor Yōmei, was the enlightened statesman who founded Japanese Buddhism. While acting as regent for Empress Suiko, Prince Shōtoku used his influence in the Japanese government. Exercising political leadership, he insisted on such measures as *Kan-i Jūnikan* (twelve cap ranks) and the seventeen-article constitution in order to centralize the government and strengthen the authority of the imperial institution. In later years, the prince devoted himself entirely to a spiritual life. After his death many legends grew around him, eventually crediting him with almost divine powers.

This set of five volumes recounts the historical story as well as the legendary life of Prince Shōtoku. Accordingly, he is variously represented as a baby praying, a young adult praying for his father's recovery, and a miraculous man who eyes emit fire and burn a wicked priest. He is shown receiving a gift of sutra from Korea, with the help of which he tries to persuade the emperor to institute days in each month when it is forbidden to kill animals. In addition he rides a horse across the sky to observe the whole country and orders the building of many temples throughout Japan. Finally, his death is followed by many miraculous events, such as the appearance of the God of Thunder and the sighting of flying fish.

The paintings and calligraphy, of the finest quality *nara-ehon*, are notable for the delicacy and variety of the figures and faces, and for the ornate costumes depicted. Nowhere can be found a better example of this work from the earlier phase of the *nara-ehon* genre of the mid-seventeenth century.

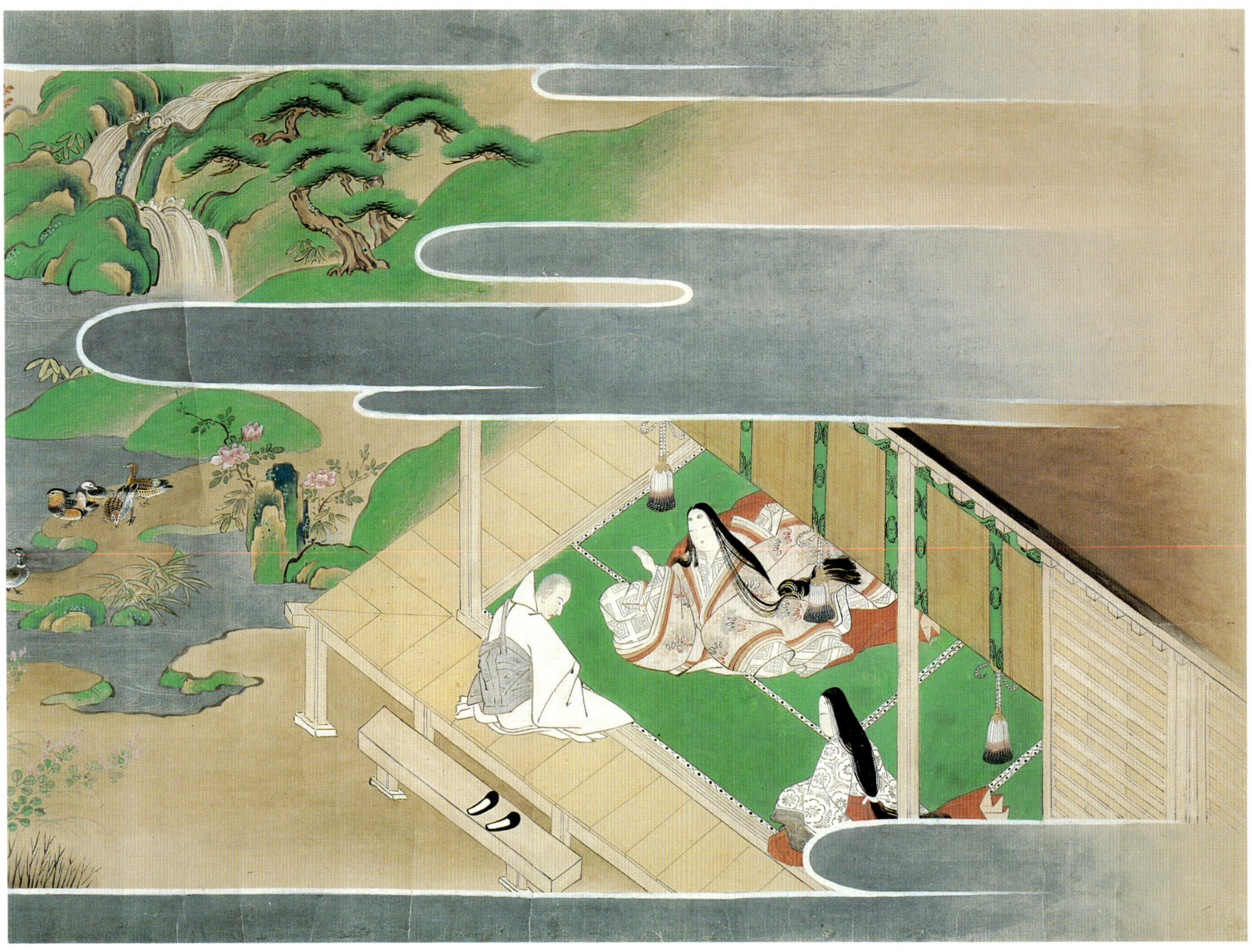

24. Zōga Shōnin is reprimanded by his mother

24.

Zōga Shōnin Gyōgōki Emaki

(The Biography of Zōga Shōnin)

Hōjuken Hōgan (dates unknown)

1711, Edo period

Two scrolls; ink, colors, silver, and gold on paper

I: H 35 L 1210; II: H 35 L 1164

CBJ No. 1130 (68)

These two scrolls tell the story of Zōga Shōnin (913–1003), a famous but eccentric Japanese Buddhist priest of the Tendai school. A Chinese text accompanies the paintings, which are of the Tosa style with some *nara-e* influence. These scrolls were specially commissioned by a priest of Shigaiji Temple in Tōno Mine Valley, where Zōga Shōnin preached for over forty years. Altogether seventeen scenes illustrate his entire life, from birth to death, in addition to a series of miraculous events that took place hundreds of years later during the Eishō period (1504–21).

In one scene, Zōga Shōnin rides an ox with a huge dried salmon in place of a sword, while in another he gives away all his clothes to the poor and walks around naked, much to the consternation of the populace. Zōga Shōnin was also a professed believer in Acalamaha, the god of fire, and in one scene he is portrayed overcoming a three-headed and eight-armed demon through the power of his prayer to this god. In accordance with his will, the remains of Zōga Shōnin's body are untouched for three years after his death. When his coffin is eventually opened, his undecomposed body is revealed still in the original posture of a praying figure.

Painted scrolls of Zōga Shōnin are extremely rare, the only other known example being the property of Tanzan Shrine in Tōno Mine Valley in Shiga prefecture, near the Kyoto district.

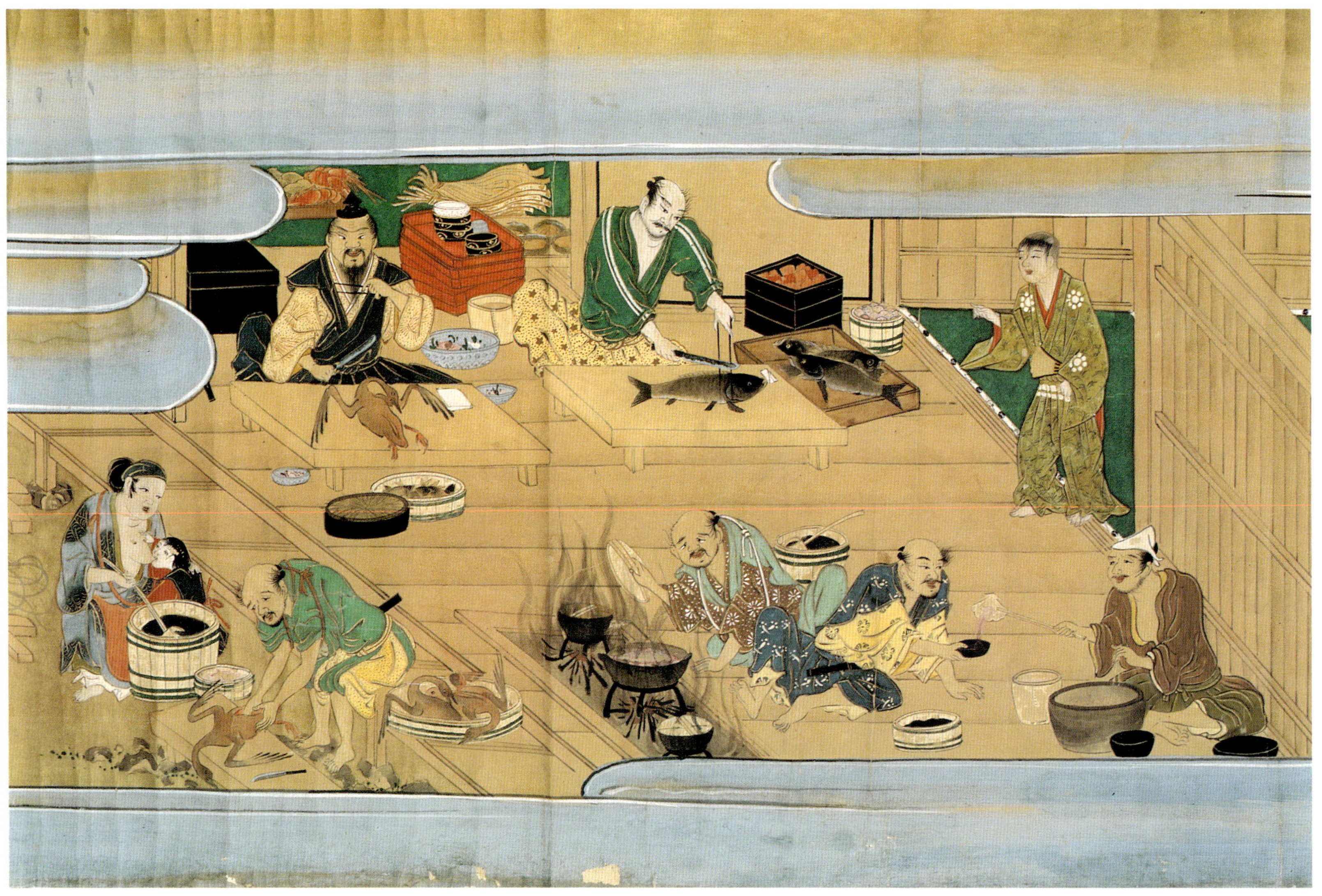

25. Discussing the merits of sake and rice

25.

Shuhanron Emaki

(Printed scroll of the debate over sake and rice)

Anonymous

Middle of 17th century, Edo period

One scroll; ink, colors, silver, and gold on paper

H 34 L 1200

CBJ No. 1121 (39)

Discussions among a heavy drinker, a poor teetotaler, and a moderate drinker are in progress. Each talks in a dignified manner about the merit of his particular habit. The heavy drinker extols the goodness and benefits of sake, drawing on examples from ancient Chinese and Japanese classical wisdom. The teetotaler stresses its ill effects and describes the virtues of eating rice instead. The third man offers the most sensible opinion: he explains that the most important factor is moderation, concluding that there is always a middle path in everything.

26.

Muramatsu Monogatari Emaki

(The Tale of Muramatsu)

Attributed to Iwasa Matabei (1578–1650)

Beginning of 17th century, Edo period

Three scrolls; ink, colors, silver, and gold on paper

I: H 32.6 L 1203; II: H 32.7 L 1209;

III: H 32.6 L 1205

CBJ No. 1127 (4)

These three scrolls from a set of twelve or more scrolls resemble *Horie Monogatari* and *Yamanaka Tokiwa Monogatari* by Iwasa Matabei, a well-known seventeenth-century painter, in the collection of the Mokichi Okada International Association in Atami, Shizuoka prefecture, in Japan. They were thought to be part of a set of twelve scrolls of the same title that were formerly housed in a collection belonging to the Matsudaira family of Echizen province (present-day Fukui prefecture) and had been on sale in 1925. It has recently been confirmed by this writer, however, that Sir Chester Beatty purchased his three scrolls in Kyoto eight years prior to the 1925 sale. (They appear on the export application list of Japanese items purchased by him in 1917.)

In comparison with the text, the painting sections are remarkably long and are characterized by copious use of gold and silver paint and gold leaf. Although in manner and composition the paintings seem to be in the style of Iwasa Matabei, according to Professor Tsuji Nobuo,,they were possibly the work of amateur artists who were following the style of Matabei.[12] The first scroll illustrates a banquet held in honor of the provincial governor of Sagami province (present-day Kanagawa prefecture). Shown at the banquet is Muramatsu, head of a powerful clan in the province. Soon afterwards Muramatsu builds a luxurious manor house to welcome the governor and his party. The second scroll depicts the governor (now married to Muramatsu's daughter) being exiled to Oki Island owing to the emperor's disapproval of his disobedience. In the third scroll, the governor's young wife, Lady Maramatsu, and her son lead a life of hardship in the northern part of Japan, where they are sold to a slave dealer who treats them cruelly.

Since these three scrolls constitute only a portion of the whole set, the narrative is of a fragmentary nature.

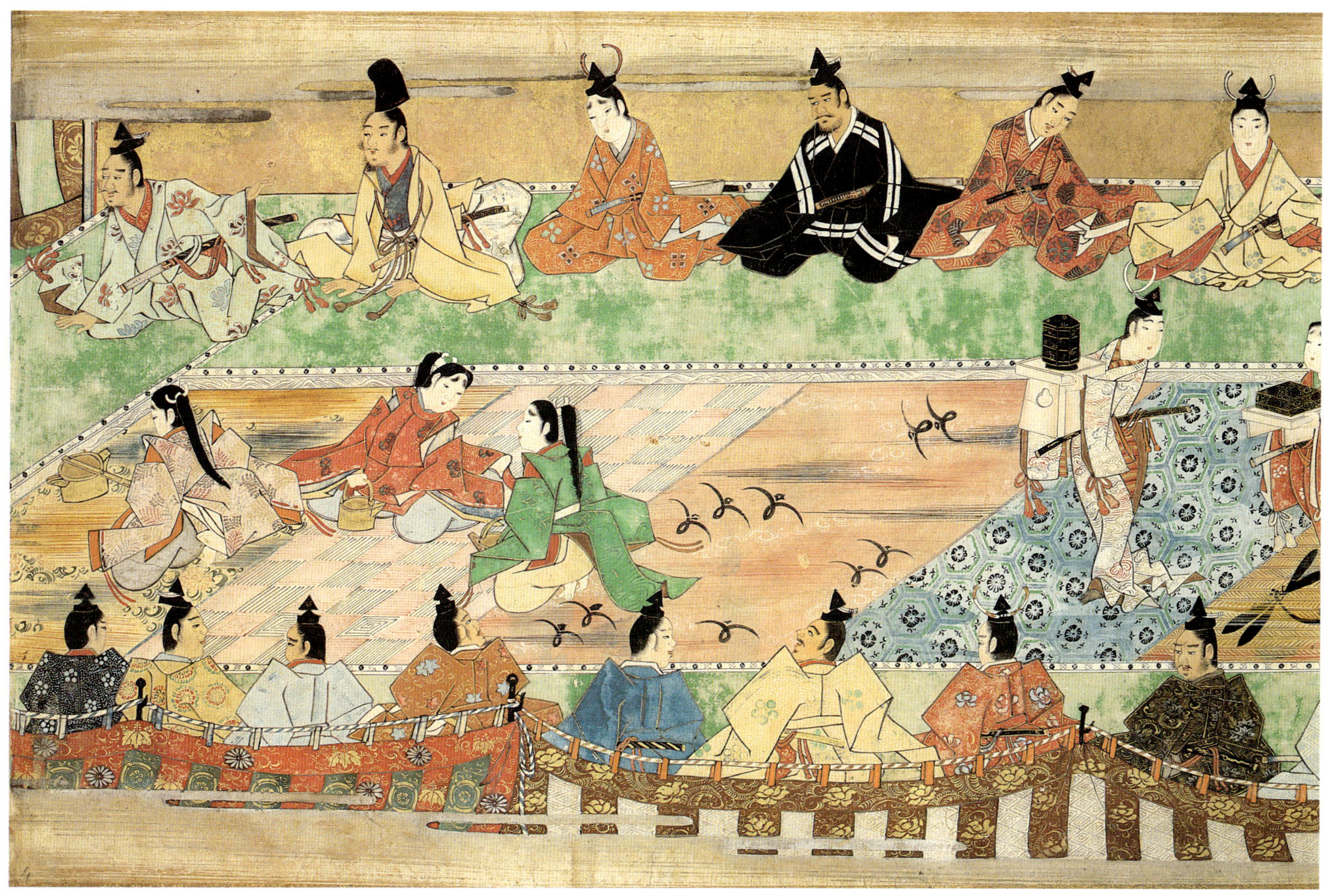

26. A banquet scene

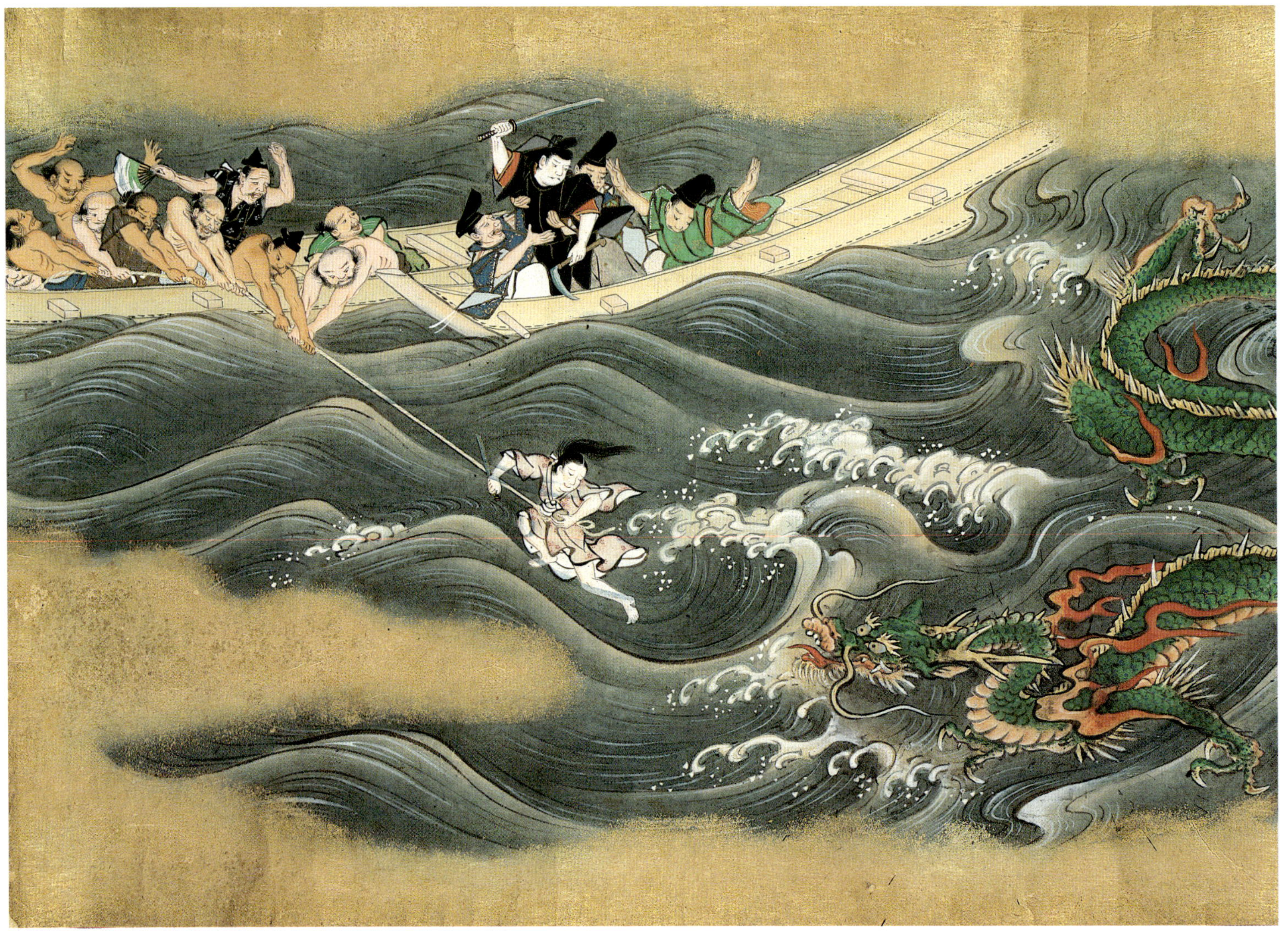

27. The attack of the sea demon

27.

Mai no Hon Emaki

(Painted scrolls of Kōwaka Mai)

Anonymous

Middle of 17th century, Edo period

Six scrolls; ink, colors, silver, and gold on paper

I: H 34 L 1575; II: H 34 L 1888;

III: H 34 L 1700; IV: H 34 L 1650;

V: H 34 L 2060; VI: H 34 L 1840

CBJ Nos. 1128, 1149 (5)

These six scrolls are apparently from a set of thirty-six scenes of Kōwaka Mai drama, a form of musical play whose themes relate mostly to fourteenth-century war stories. The origins of Kōwaka Mai are not certain. First records of it appeared in the mid-fifteenth century, when the Kōwaka family of Echizen province (present-day Fukui prefecture) began to claim to be leading exponents of the form. Today, Kōwaka Mai is performed only in the small village of Ōe in Fukuoka prefecture. Although both Noh theater and Kōwaka Mai seem to have been equally enjoyed by war lords during the sixteenth and seventeenth centuries, Kōwaka Mai suffered a sudden decline in popularity early in the seventeenth century, most likely owing to its less refined and more rustic tone. Despite this fall in favor, the literary influence of Kōwaka Mai has survived, especially in the narrative scrolls and albums commonly known as *nara-ehon*.

In terms of painting and calligraphy, these six scrolls are of the finest quality. They were probably produced as a set for presentation to a daimyō (lord), and they comprise the following stories: "Yuriwaka" (13 illustrations), "Taishokuhan" (11 illustrations), "Kagekiyo" (9 illustrations), "Takadachi" (14 illustrations), "Fushimi Tokiwa" (9 illustrations), "Tokiwa Mondou" (5 illustrations), "Fue no Maki" (5 illustrations), "Tsurugi Sandan" (6 illustrations), and "Miraiki" (5 illustrations).[13] Of these, "Taishokuhan" and "Fushimi Tokiwa" were especially popular.

"Taishokuhan" (the great woven cap) was originally the title given to the person who held the highest rank at court, but it later became associated with Fujiwara no Kamatari (614–699), the founder of the powerful and noble Fujiwara clan.

According to the story, Kamatari's beautiful daughter is summoned by the Chinese emperor to the T'ang court to live as his consort. Kamatari is beginning the construction of Kōfukuji Temple in Nara, and his daughter sends gifts from China for its decoration. On the way, one of the gifts, a most precious jewel, is stolen by the Dragon King's daughter. Kamatari travels to the coast where the jewel has been lost. There he meets a woman diver; they become lovers and she bears him a son. She is persuaded by Kamatari to dive underwater to recover the stolen jewel. Although she manages to retrieve the gem, she is attacked by the fierce dragon and tries in vain to escape, while the men aboard the ship attempt to rescue her. Among the agitated courtiers is Kamatari himself, holding a sickle and preparing to leap into the sea to save her.

The story goes that the dragon attacks the woman with its claws, but she cuts open her own chest and inserts the gem within it. When her body washes ashore, the jewel is found inside the wound. Kamatari later embeds it in the forehead of the statue of Buddha at Kōfukuji Temple.

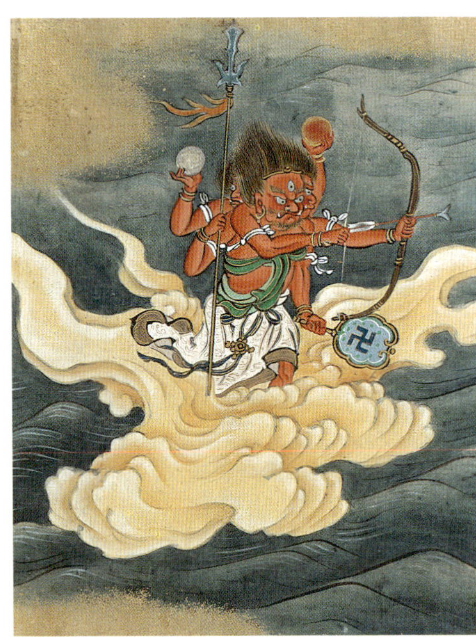

27. The God of Thunder

The other popular story tells of Fushimi Tokiwa, daughter of Fujiwara no Koremitsu, and one of the most beautiful and charming ladies of her time. Such is her beauty that Minamoto no Yoshitomo, war lord of the Minamoto clan, takes her as his concubine. She bears him three sons: Imawaka, Otowaka, and Ushiwaka, who later becomes known as the famous Yoshitsune (see cat. nos. 13 and 14). In the year of Ushiwaka's birth, 1159, Yoshitomo attacks and burns the palace of Emperor Goshirakawa during the absence of Taira no Kiyomori, war lord of the Taira clan. Taira no Kiyomori later sends his son Shigemori to exact revenge, whereupon Yoshitomo is defeated and flees to Owari (present-day Aichi prefecture). His house is then attacked and set on fire.

Narrowly escaping, Tokiwa flees through the deep snow in search of safety, taking with her the three boys. The youngest, Ushiwaka, is but an infant still at her breast. Tokiwa's flight with her children has proven to be a favorite subject for Japanese artists, and few stories in Japanese history have inspired more pity than the desperate plight of Tokiwa making this weary journey, trailing bloodstains in the snow from her bare and frozen feet.

When she reaches the Yoshino Mountains, Tokiwa is stopped by the guard Munekiyo at the security post of Fushimi and is compelled to surrender to Taira no Kiyomori so that her children's lives may be spared. Hearing of the assassination of Yoshitomo in February 1160, she travels to Rokuhara, the headquarters of the Heike clan, and surrenders herself to Kiyomori, imploring him to release her aged mother and to have mercy on her children. The price demanded of her is that she become his concubine, for she is still only twenty-five years old and her beauty delights Kiyomori. Her captive mother is duly released. Unable to tolerate the presence of the children, however, Kiyomori has the two older boys sent off to a temple to be trained as priests, while Ushiwaka is left in his mother's care only until he turns seven.

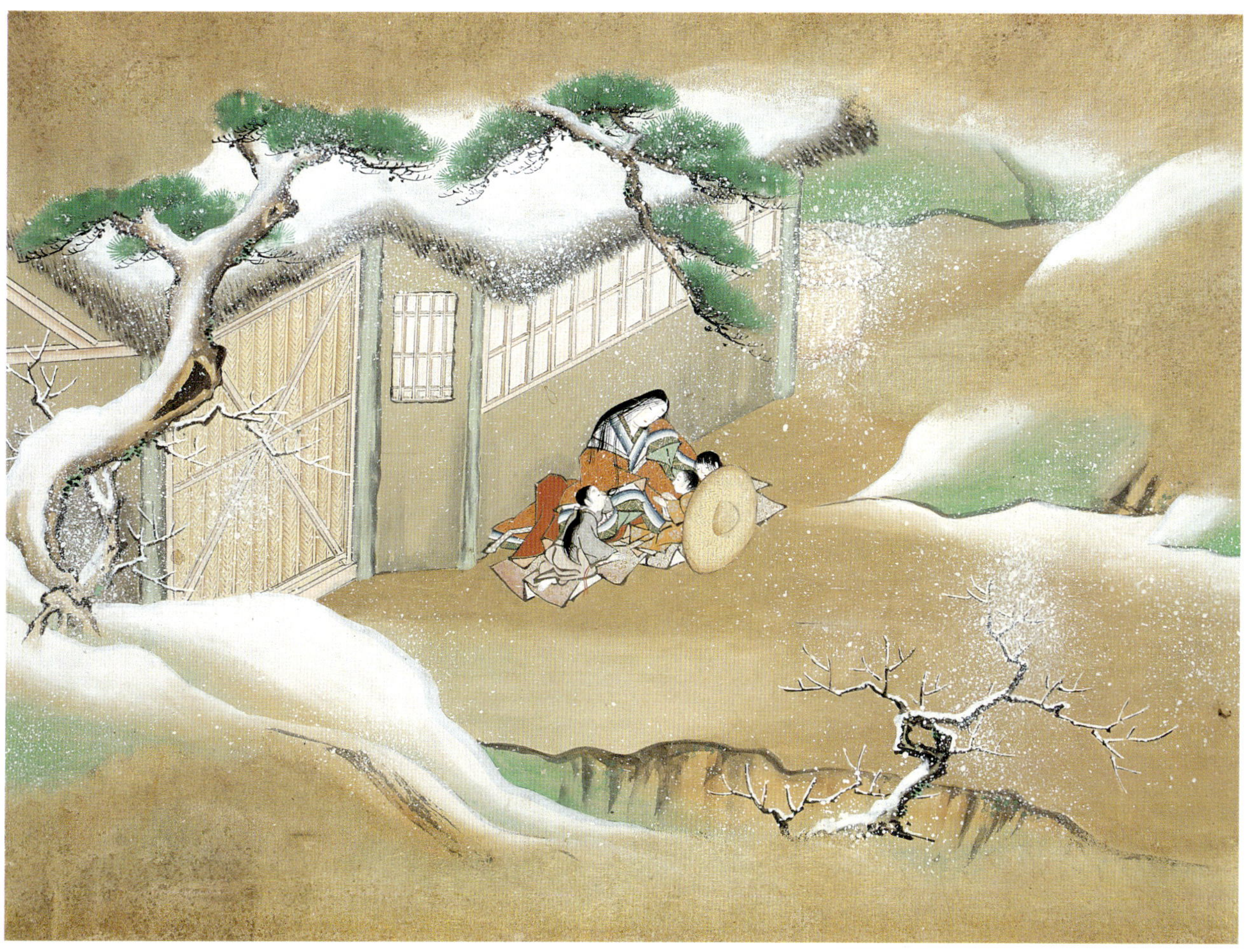

27. Fushimi Tokiwa protects her children

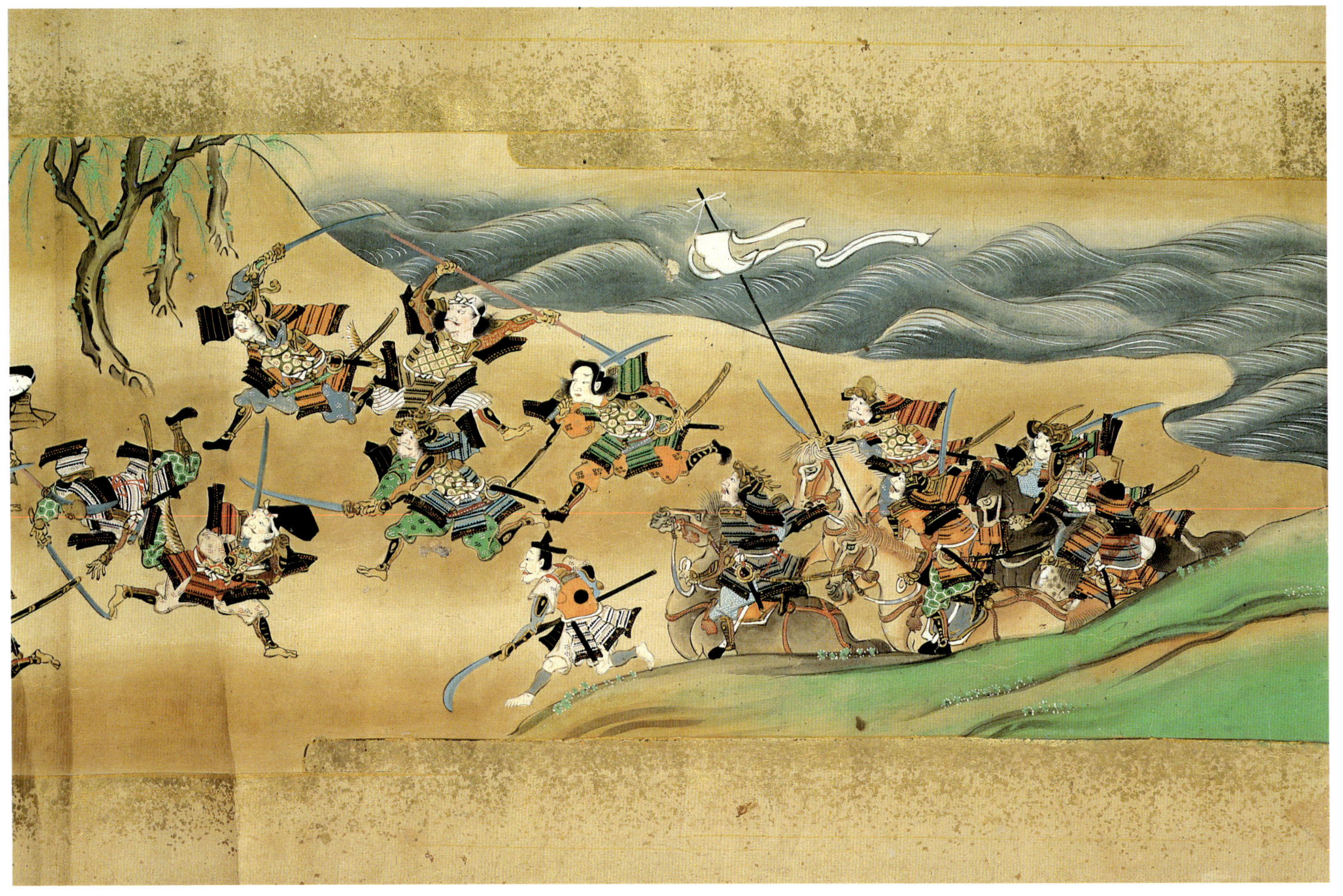

28. Hangaku in battle

28.

Eshima Monogatari Emaki

(The Tale of Princess Eshima)

Anonymous

Middle of 17th century, Edo period

One scroll; ink, colors, and gold on paper

H 32.5 L 1547

CBJ No. 1124 (13)

Originating from a set of two scrolls, this work depicts a thirteenth-century romance involving Princess Eshima and a famous warrior from eastern Japan. It also tells the story of a female warrior named Hangaku, who is the mother of Princess Eshima. Together with her daughter, Hangaku fights desperately against Shinkai Kōshirō, a warrior who has killed her husband. Hangaku is also renowned for her bravery is assisting her nephew, the warrior Sukemori, in his armed campaign against the Minamoto clan, Yoriie.

The paintings and calligraphy exhibit the finest quality among *nara-ehon,* which is characterized by stylized mists and clouds in gold at the top and bottom of the scroll.

29.

Chōgonka Emaki
(Song of Everlasting Regret)
Kanō Sansetsu (1590–1651)
17th century, Edo period
Two scrolls; ink, colors, silver, and gold on silk
I: H 33 L 1046; II: H 33 L 1097
CBJ No. 1158 (87)

The well-known Chinese legend of Yang Kuei-fei (719–756) greatly influenced Heian literature in Japan. The tragic love story about the Chinese emperor and his beloved concubine was originally written as a long epic poem by the renowned poet Bai Juyi (772–846).

These scrolls consist of thirty-five scenes that are minutely painted in full color on silk with touches of gold and silver. Unfortunately, no text accompanies the poems, but the epic story can be traced from the detailed paintings. Although the scrolls bear the signature of Kanō Sansetsu, that authenticity is arguable. The typical style of the Kanō school is readily observed in the paintings, in particular in the depiction of the rugged grandeur of the mountains and in the aged trees. Yet the paintings lack some strength and vitality, perhaps, as Professor Wakisaka Atsushi has suggested, due to the delicacy of the silk material and the miniature scale of painting.[14]

These were thought to be the only existing painted scrolls of this epic Chinese story, although there must have been some original paintings that Kanō Sansetsu had copied. The only other example of paintings of this story was in fact mentioned in 1893 in the Japanese art magazine *Kokka* (no. 44). The paintings in question, however, were done on paper rather than silk and in ink with light colors. Until 1988, the existence of these scrolls belonging to the Kuki family in Kobe city was not known. According to Professor Wakisaka, they are very similar in composition to the Chester Beatty scrolls, but are greatly inferior in quality of painting.

The story, which is based on the epic poem, is a simple tragic tale of love. The emperor's beloved concubine Yang Kuei-fei is promoted in rank to second only to that of the empress, and the court is soon filled with her family and relations. Her father is given a good position, and her family is showered with honors. Recklessly neglecting the affairs of state, the emperor becomes addicted to senseless debauchery, while stringent taxes are imposed on the people to help fill the depleted treasury. Eventually a revolt is led by An Lushan, a former boon companion of the emperor, and the emperor is separated from his concubine during the turmoil. Yang Kuei-fei is subsequently killed. Some time afterwards, the emperor becomes aware of the presence of his beloved in heaven, and he sends a message to her through his court astrologer, requesting her to send him one of her hairpins by way of reply. With the hairpin he is said to have taken his own life. Although it is not supported by historical fact, this final part of the story is nevertheless dramatically depicted in the paintings.

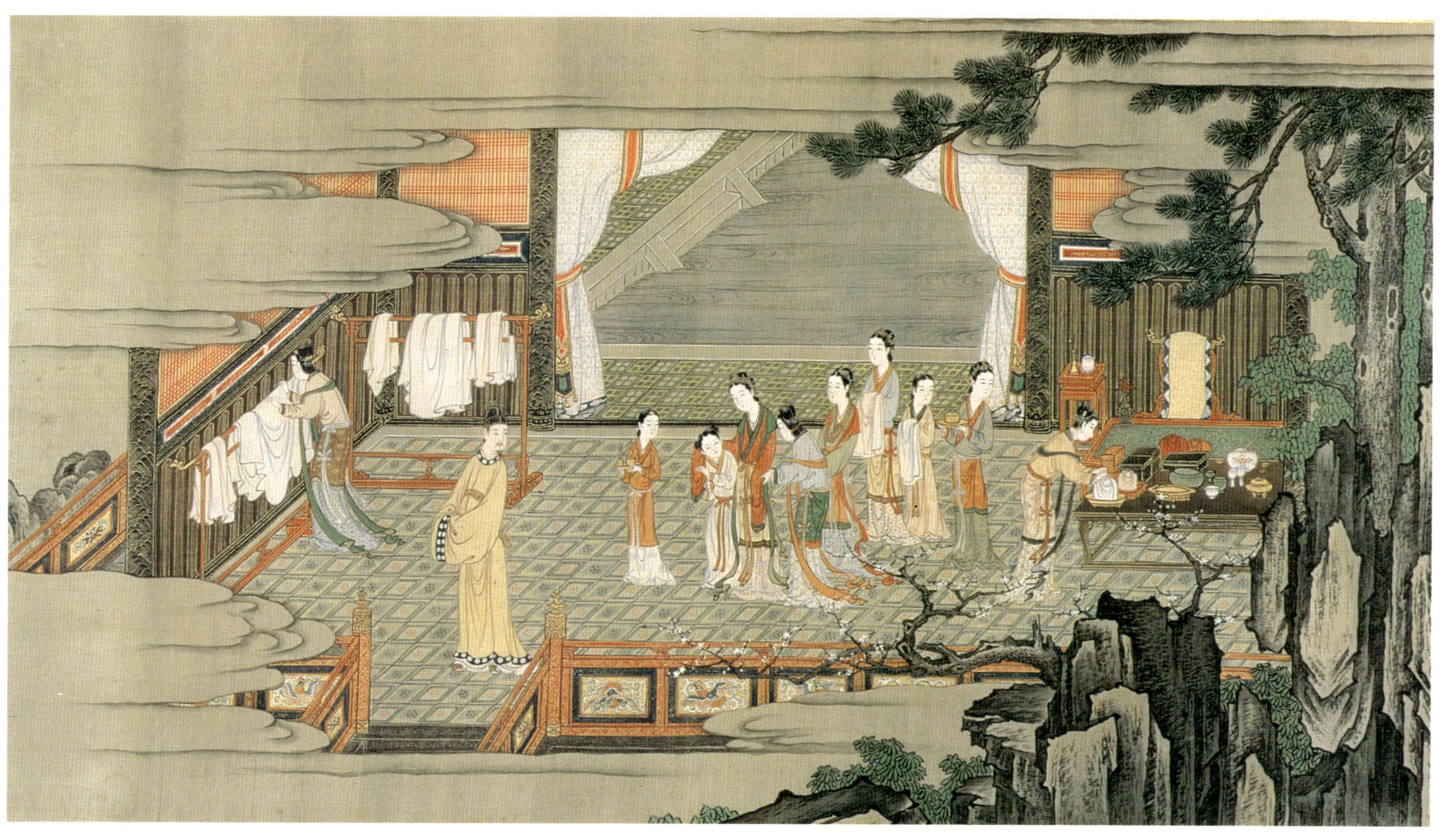

29. The emperor meets Yang Kuei-fei

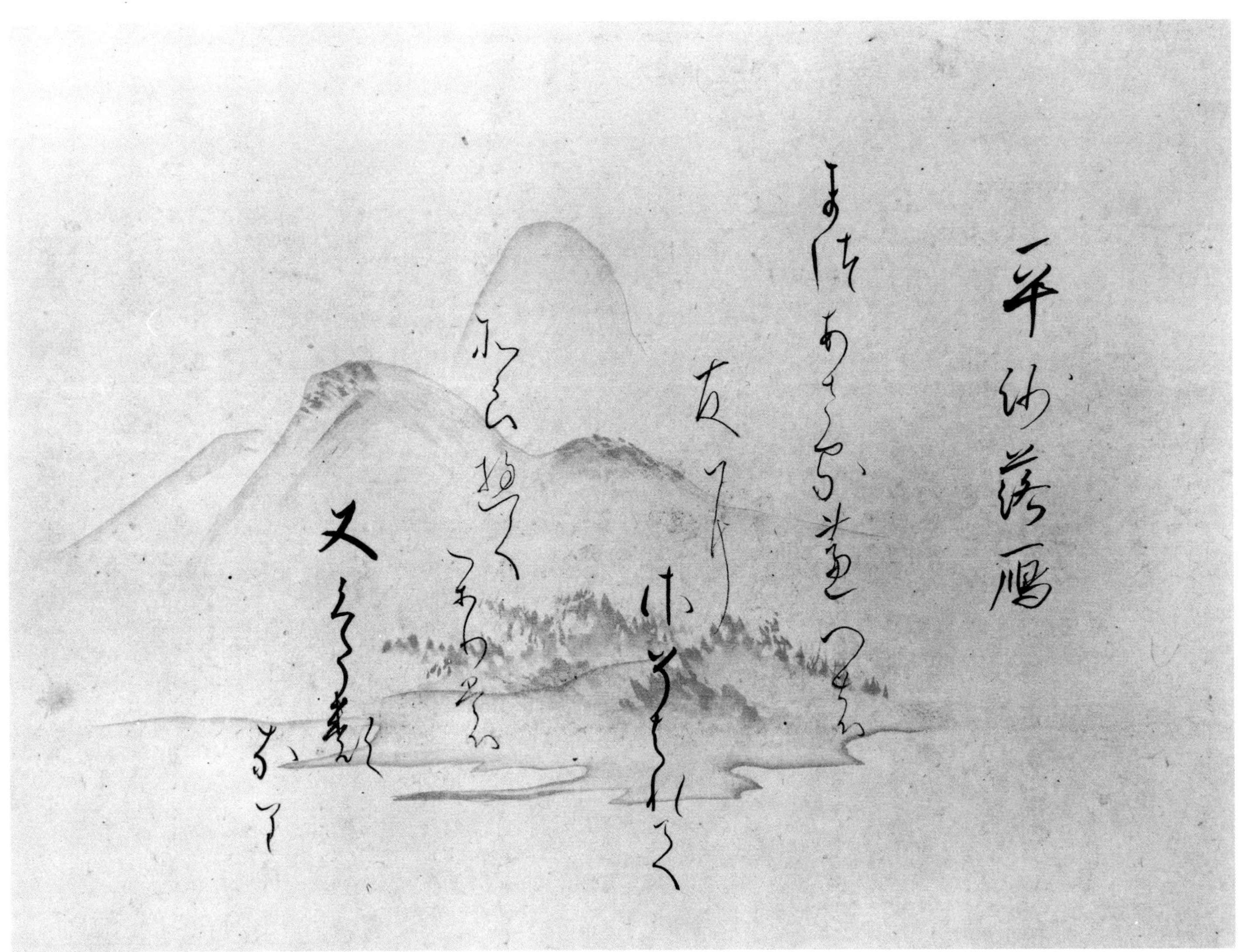

30.

30.

Shōshō Hakkei Gakan

(Eight views of the Xiao and Xiang)

Kanō Eishin (1613–1685) and others

1684, Edo period

One scroll; ink on silk

H 27 L 534

CBJ No. 1175 (77)

Eight painters from the Kanō school, among them Eishin, Tanshin, Tansetsu, Tōun, Tsunenobu, and Tanyū, each painted in ink on one silk scroll a view of the Xiao and Xiang, an acclaimed scenic spot in China. The eight paintings are accompanied by *waka* poems, similarly written by eight different calligraphers.

The eight views of the Xiao and Xiang were chosen for their picturesque scenery. Painting eight views was a particular mode of artistically treating a location of spectacular beauty, and a set sequence of subjects and features was commonly adopted.

Shūgetsu–autumn moon
Sekishō–evening glow
Banshō–evening bell
Bosetsu–evening snow
Yau–night rain
Kihan–returning boats
Seiran–clear sky
Rakugan–homeward geese

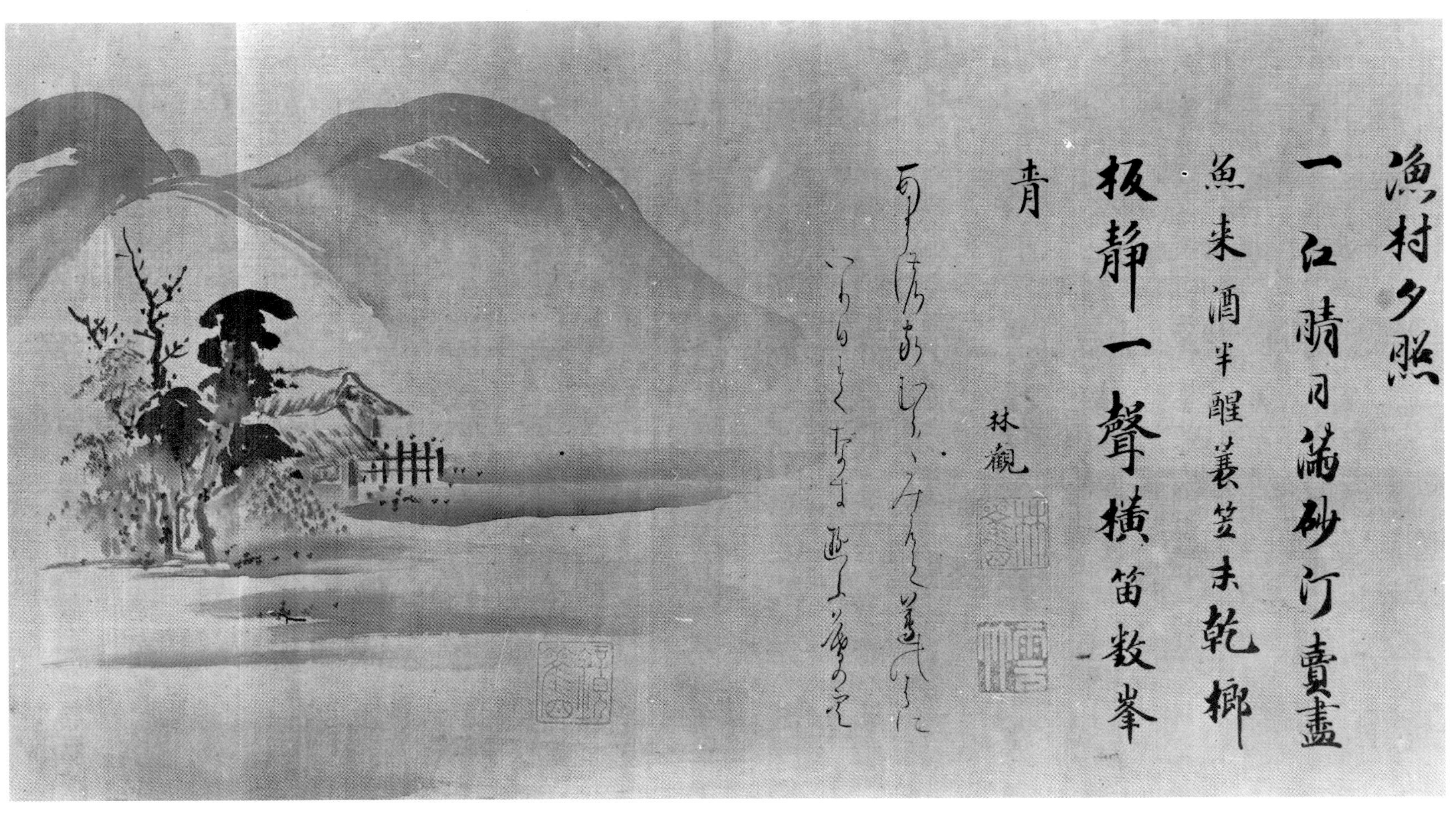

31.

31.

Shōshō Hakkei Shiika Gakan

(Eight views of the Xiao and Xiang, with poems)

Kaihō Yūchiku (1654–1728)

Beginning of 18th century, Edo period

One scroll; ink and light colors on silk

H 25 L 589

CBJ No. 1143 (90)

Here, ink paintings on a silk scroll, with some use of faint colors, depict eight views of the Xiao and Xiang. The accompanying poems appear in both Chinese and Japanese, a feature that is quite unique in a scroll of this genre. The paintings were all executed by Kaihō Yūchiku, while the calligraphy is the work of eight different hands, among them Taikyoan, Rinkan, and Unchiku.

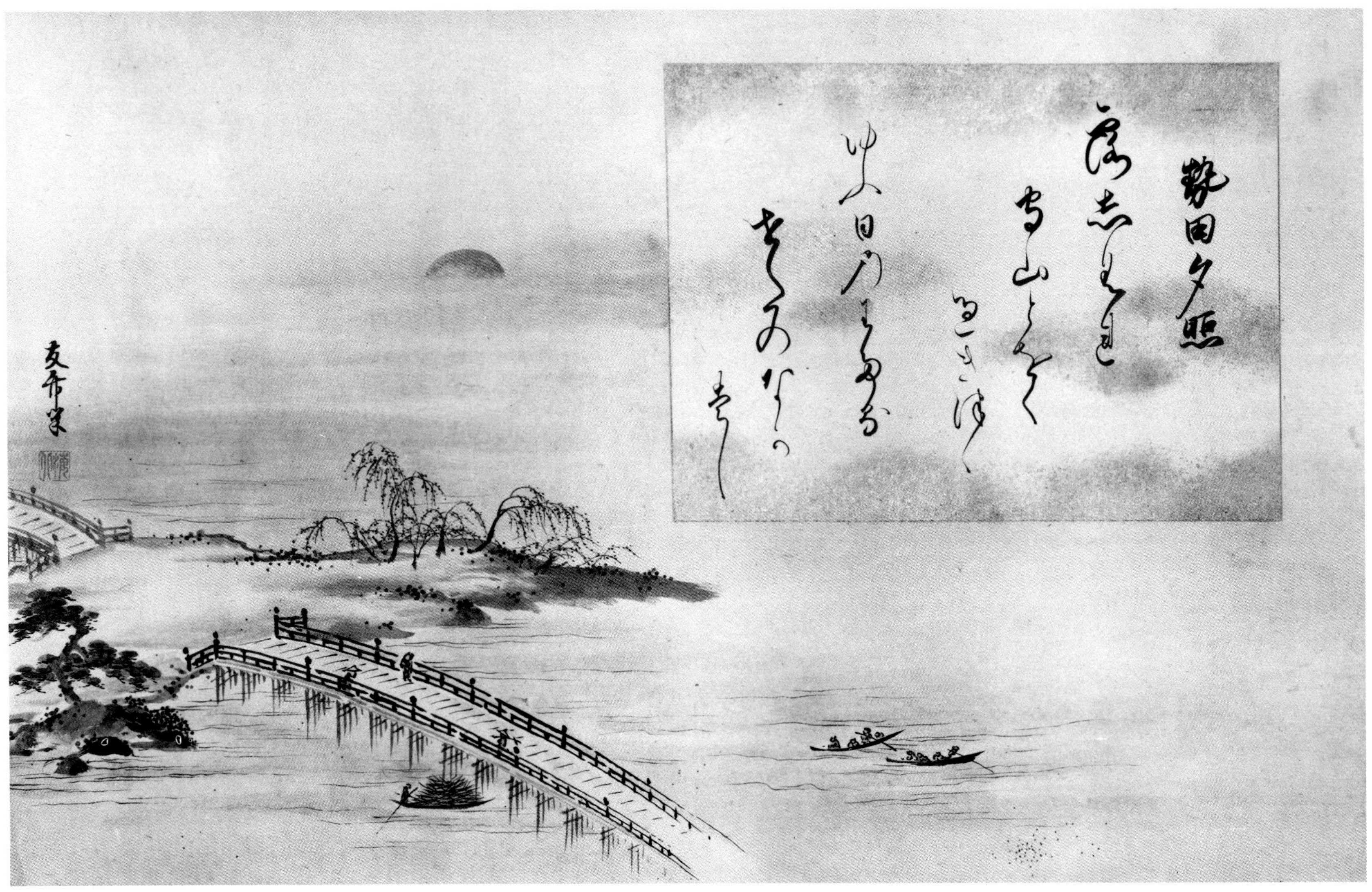

32.

32.
Ōmi Hakkei Gakan
(Eight views of Ōmi)
Kaihō Yūchiku (1654–1728)
Beginning of 18th century, Edo period
One scroll; ink and light colors on paper
H 30.4 L 381
CBJ No. 1140 (91)

Eight views of Ōmi, in present-day Shiga prefecture, near Kyoto, follow the same sequence as those of the Xiao and Xiang (see cat. nos. 30 and 31). Painted in light colors, each view is accompanied by an appropriate *waka* poem.

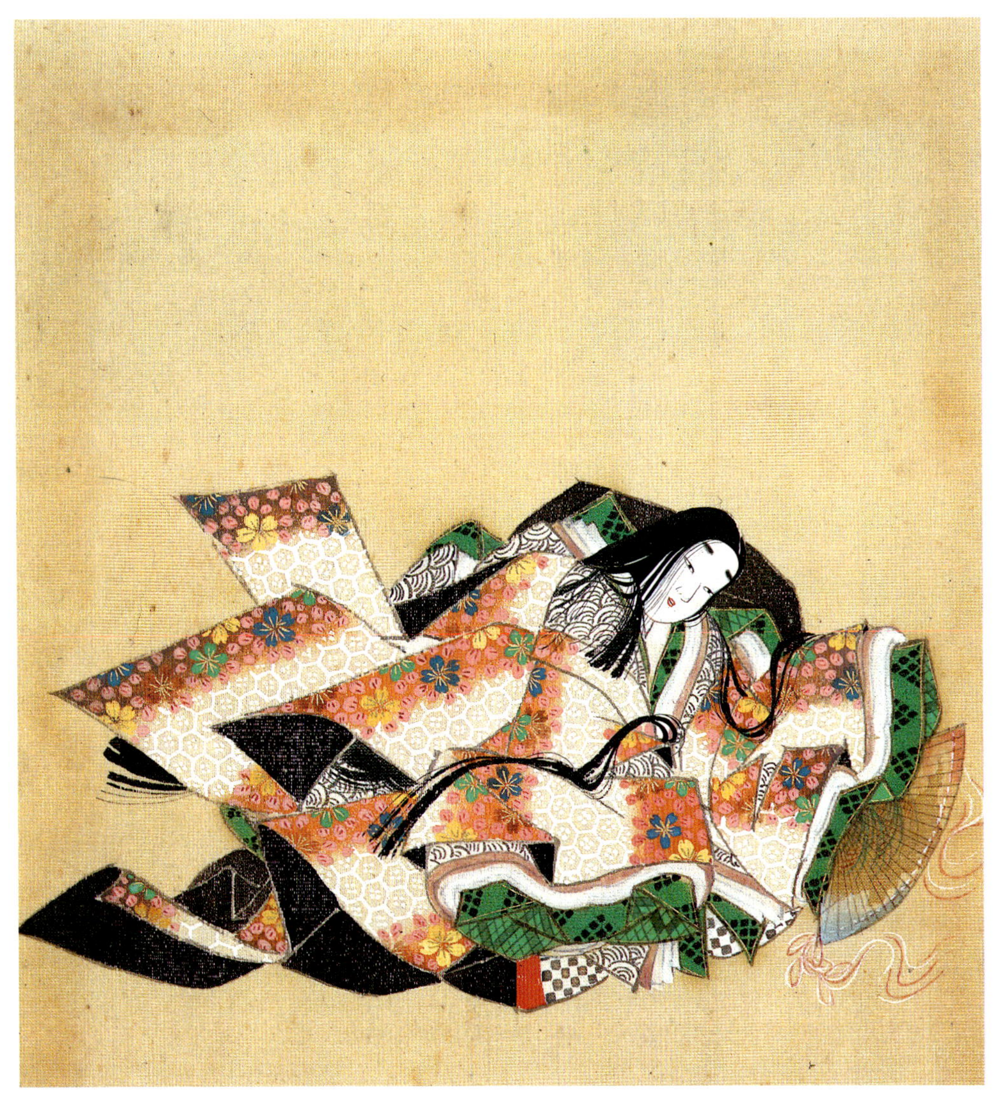

33.

33.

Sanjūrokkasen Gajō

(The Thirty-six Immortals of Japanese Poetry)

Sumiyoshi Jokei (1631–1705)

Middle of 17th century, Edo period

One volume; ink, colors, silver, and gold on silk

H 24.3 W 19.8

CBJ No. 1008 (64)

Japanese books of paintings and calligraphy are often bound in a concertina-type album with sheets of *shikishi* (literally, colored paper) affixed to the folds.

The subject is a traditional one: the Thirty-six Immortals of Japanese Poetry. The chosen thirty-six poets and examples of their poems were assembled in the Heian period and have been the theme of elegant album-making ever since. In particular, they were a favorite subject of the Tosa school of painters. Many albums containing portraits of the immortal poets have survived from the Edo period. This is one example, with poems and portraits appearing on facing pages. Each poem sheet includes the poet's name, his or her position in the contesting Left and Right groups, and one representative poem. The first portrait is that of Hitomaro, while the last is that of Nakatsukasa. Each poem sheet is adorned with decorative motifs and designs.

All thirty-six portraits were delicately painted in bright colors and stylized forms by Sumiyoshi Jokei, who was also known as Hirozumi.

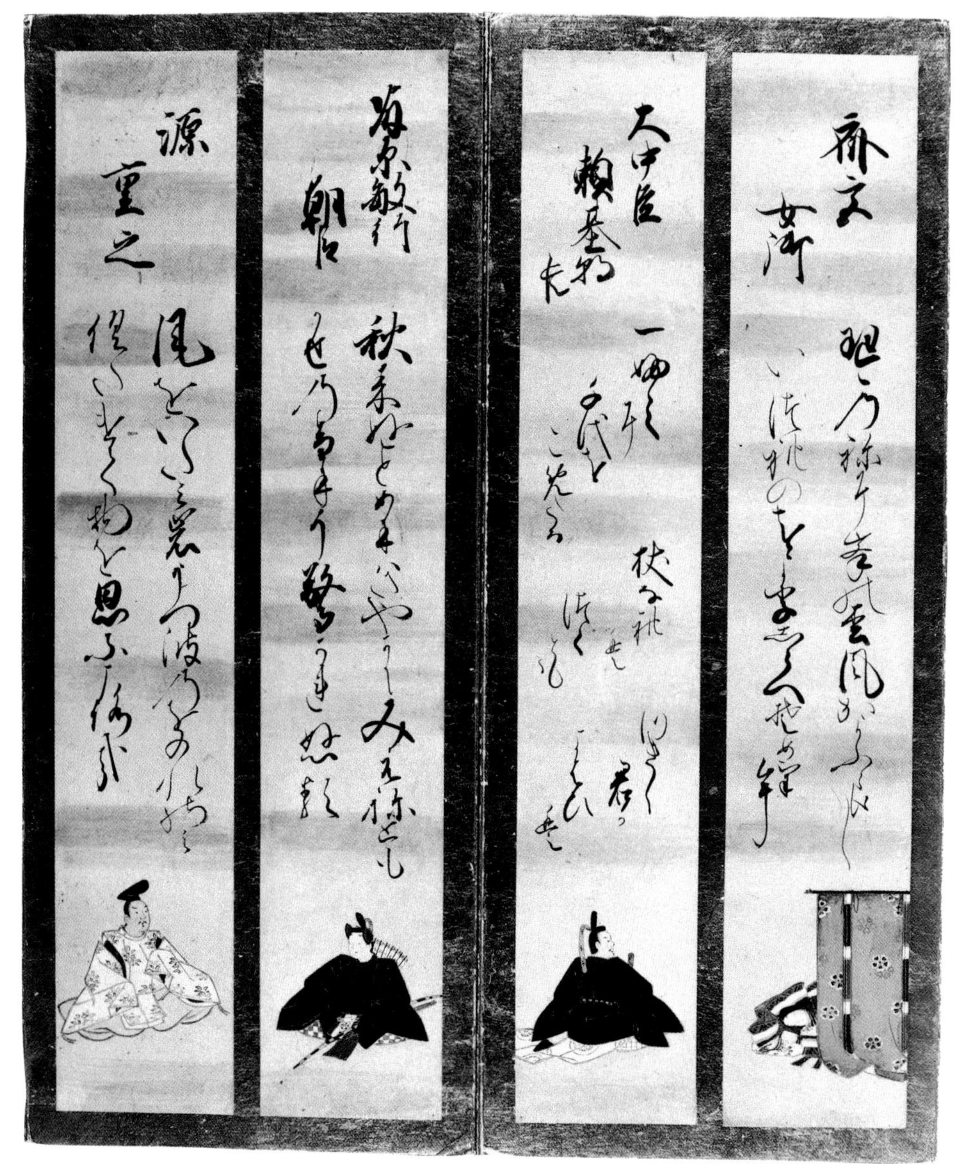

34.

34.

Sanjūrokkasen Tanzaku Gajō

(The Thirty-six Immortals of Japanese Poetry)

Anonymous

End of 17th century, Edo period

One album; ink, colors, and gold on silk

H 39 W 15.8

CBJ No. 1012 (66)

Written on *tanzaku,* a special sheet of elegant paper used for writing poems, this concertina-type album holds a collection of portraits of the Thirty-six Immortal Poets and their representative poems. The portraits of the poets are painted in the lower part of the *tanzaku,* with their representative poems above them. Each page contains two *tanzaku,* representing a poet from the Left group and one from the Right.

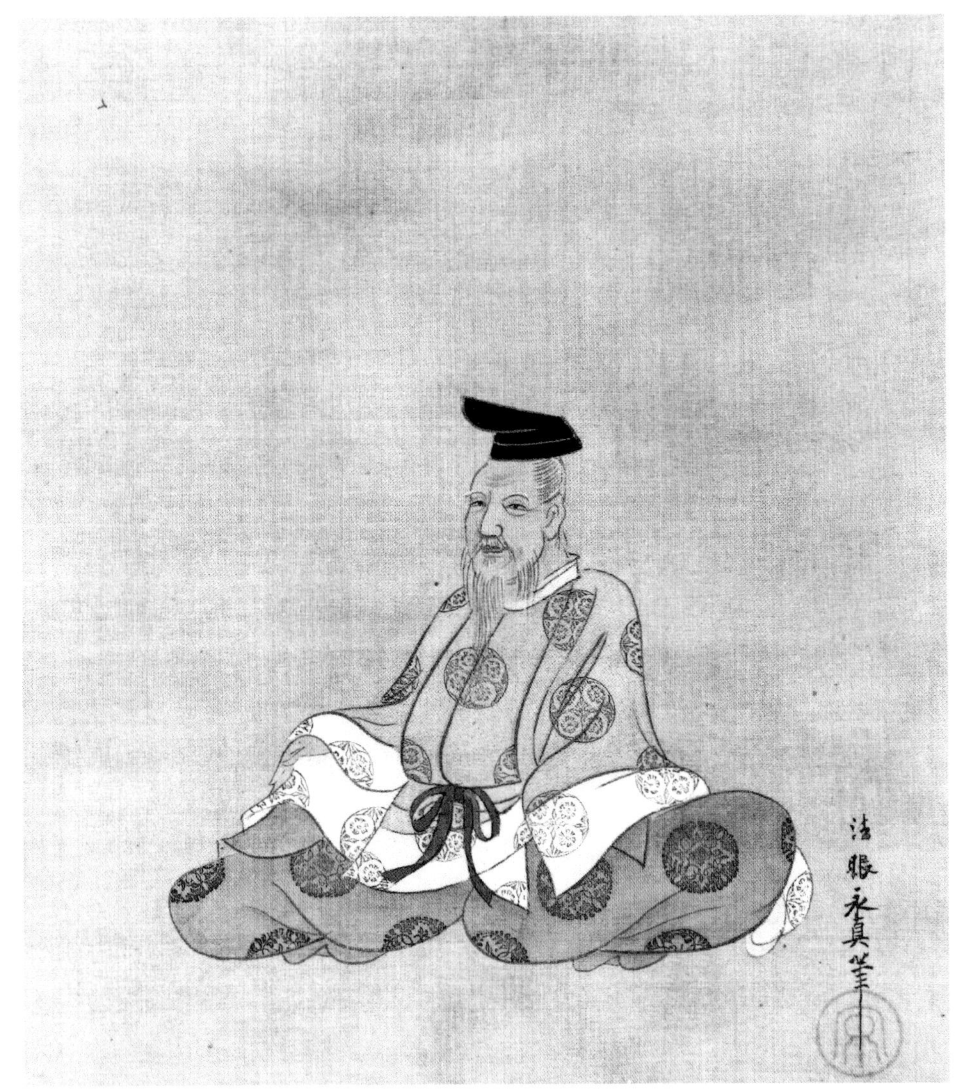

35.

35.

Sanjūrokkasen Gajō

(The Thirty-six Immortals of Japanese Poetry)

Kanō Eishin (1613–1685), Kanō Tokinobu (1642–1678)

Middle of 17th century, Edo period

One album; ink, colors, and gold on silk

H 25.1 L 21.5

CBJ No. 1030 (76)

The poems are written on the righthand side of open pages of *shikishi* paper, with the poets' portraits painted on the lefthand side on silk. The first four portraits are by Kanō Eishin, while the remainder are signed by his adopted son Tokinobu.

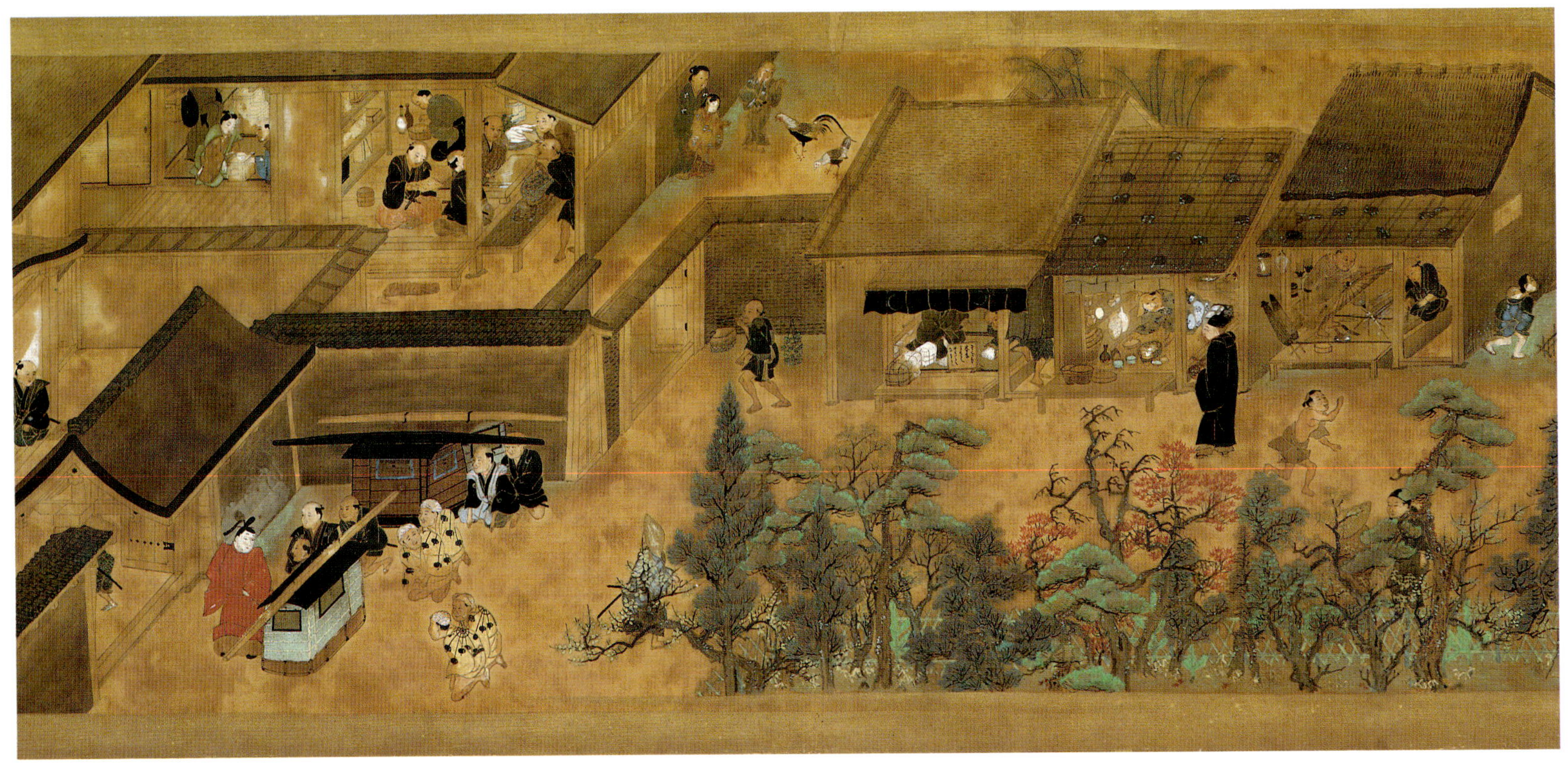

36.

36.

Tohi Zukan

(Painted scroll of scenes in and around Kyoto)

Sumiyoshi Jokei (1631–1705)

End of 17th century, Edo period

One scroll; ink, colors, silver, and gold on silk

H 30.4 L 1262

CBJ No. 1120 (63)

Produced in full color on silk, these Tosa-style paintings by Sumiyoshi Jokei show various activities and street scenes taking place in Kyoto in spring and summer in the first part of the scroll. Pastoral country scenes from autumn and winter fill the scroll's latter part. Sumiyoshi Jokei's distinctive style is manifest in the delicate touches of miniature detail that characterize his technique.

Two more scrolls on the same subject by this artist are in existence: one in the Tokyo National Museum and the other in Kōfukuin Temple in Nara. According to Sakakibara Satoru, the Chester Beatty work was probably the last of the three to be painted, since it lacks some vitality and detail in the depiction of the people in Kyoto and the country scenes.[15] The scroll was purchased by Sir Chester Beatty at the sale of the Okamura collection in Kyoto in 1917. Not only is this a valuable historical document of Kyoto, but it also stands out as an excellent example of the paintings of the Tosa genre. The scroll was completely restored in 1988.

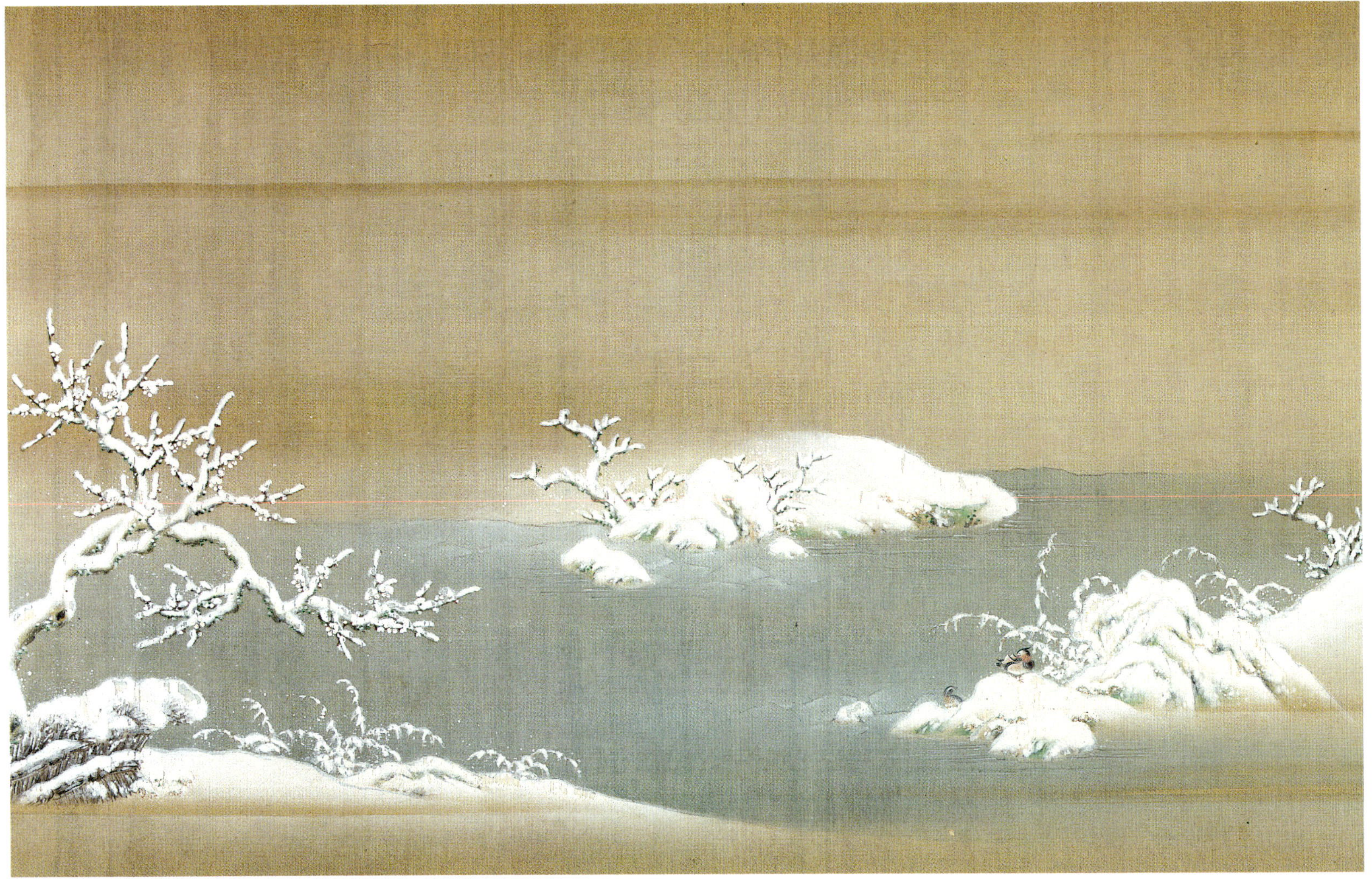

37.

37.

Fūbutsu Zukan

(Paintings of seasonal scenery)

Sumiyoshi Hiromori (1705–1777)

Middle of 18th century, Edo period

One scroll; ink, colors, and gold on silk

H 30 L 321

CBJ No. 1184 (71)

Painted in light colors on silk, the scroll shows five seasonal scenes from August to December.

August—Japanese bushclover *(hagi)* and geese

September—eulalia *(susuki)* and quails

October—chrysanthemums and cranes

November—loquats and plovers

December—aged plum trees and mandarin ducks in snow

These subjects are related to the sequence *Flowers and Birds of the Twelve Months,* paintings that accompany the poetry of Fujiwara Sadaie (Teika) (1162–1241), renowned as one of Japan's greatest poets.

Without doubt there must have been a companion scroll depicting scenes from spring and summer.

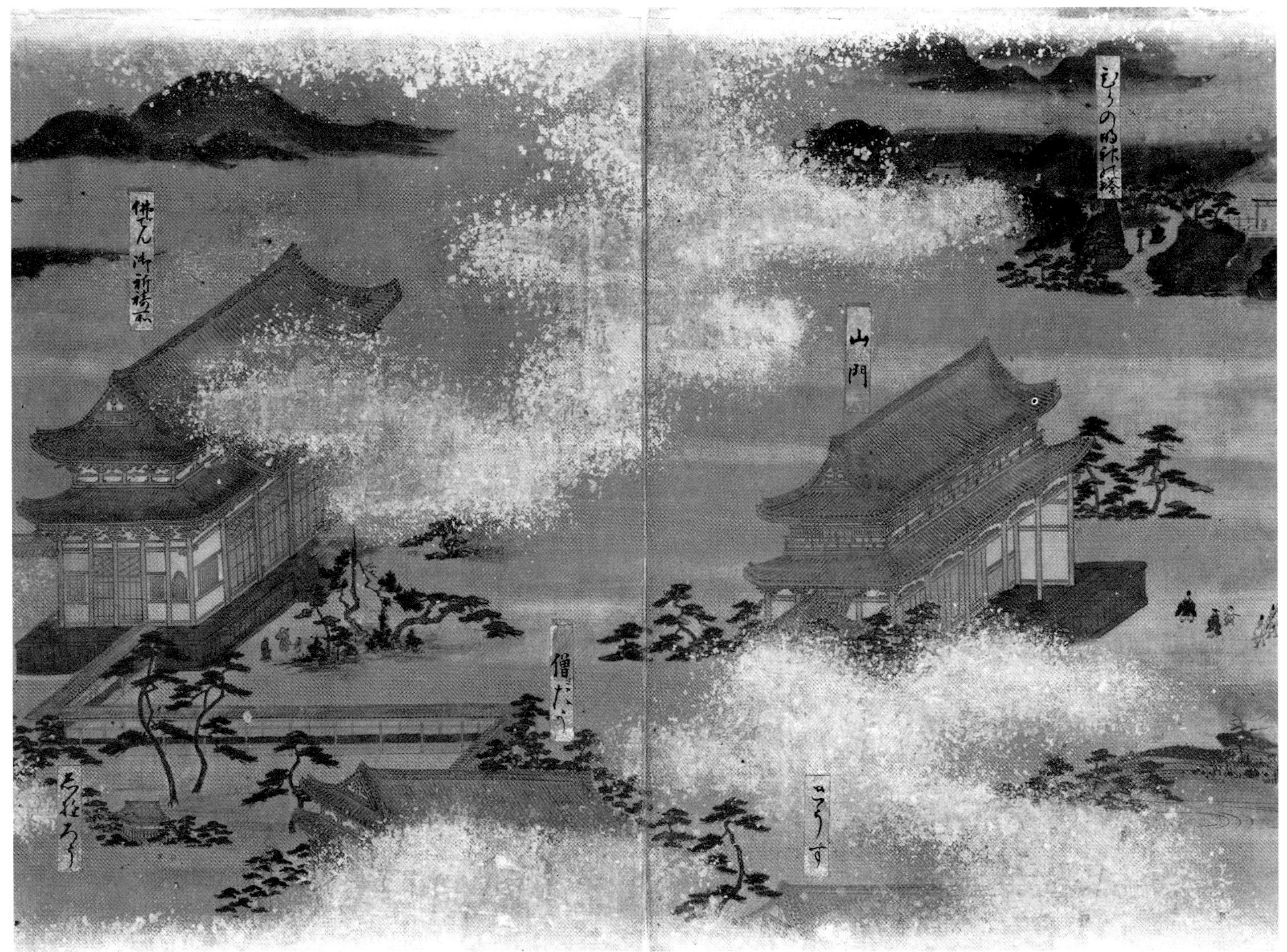

38.

38.

Kyō Tōfukuji Keidai no Zu

(Painted album of Tōfukuji Temple)

Tosa Mitsutaka (1675–1710)

End of 17th century, Edo period

One album; ink, colors, silver, and gold on silk

H 39.7 W 28

CBJ No. 1005 (67)

In this concertina-style album of twelve pages (six folded double pages), a panoramic view of a Buddhist temple is painted on silk in the traditional Tosa manner. The album shows the precincts of the Zen Buddhist Tōfukuji Temple in Kyoto, with the name of each building and occasionally its function added on a small gold label. The dark brown silk and colors have been well preserved; the gold used for the drifting clouds that intersperse the scenes has also lasted unusually well.

Mitsutaka was the name used by the painter Mitsusuke in his early years. He was a grandson of Tosa Mitsuoki, the most important artist of the Tosa school.

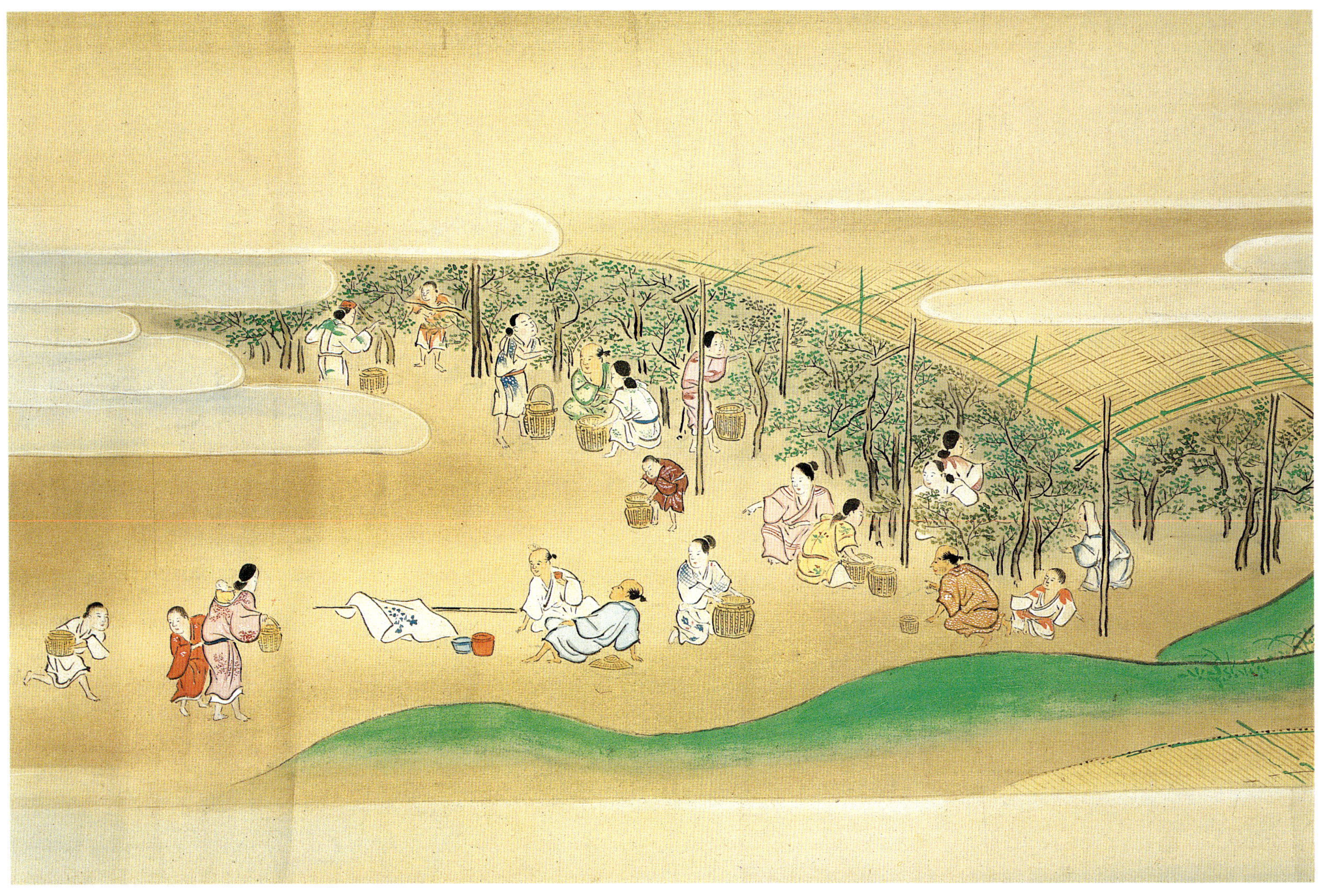

39.

39.

Uji Chatsumi Zukan

(Painted scroll of the tea harvest at Uji)

Kanō Tansetsu (1655–1714)

Beginning of 18th century, Edo period

One scroll; ink, colors, and gold on paper

H 32 L 494

CBJ No. 1137 (81)

Paintings of refined quality in light colors show the entire process of the tea industry for which the Uji district is still famous. A bridge over the Uji River, willow trees, a windmill, and silk-bleaching *(habutae)* in the river form the sequence of subjects commonly followed in depicting scenes of this site. The activities of young and old people on the tea plantations are portrayed in minute fashion, while the special technique used for making high-quality tea is shown in elaborate detail.

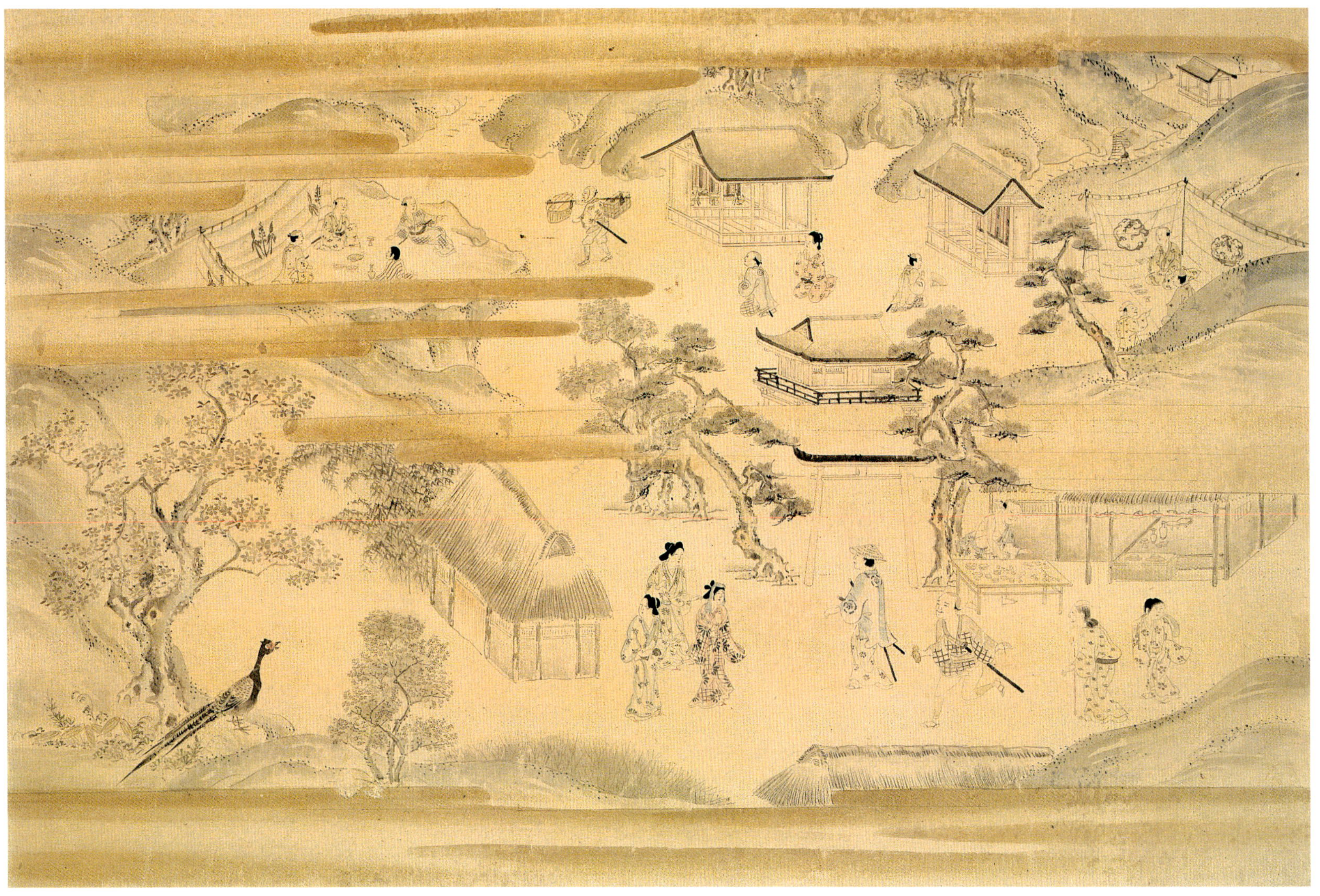

40.

40.

Jūnikagetsu Emaki

(Painted scroll of the twelve months)

Anonymous

End of 17th century, Edo period

One scroll; ink and light colors on paper

H 33.5 L 1194

CBJ No. 1112 (55)

Twelve scenes are painted on paper in an elegant grisaille manner with light touches of color. Each scene is accompanied by the name of a seasonal flower and an appropriate poem. The paper for the text is tastefully decorated with sprinkled gold and designs of flowers and grasses in faint colors of blue, pink, and yellow. This scroll is most likely based on the motifs of *Flowers and Birds of the Twelve Months,* paintings that complement the poetry of the renowned poet Fujiwara Sadaie (Teika), since the poems of this scroll are the very same. The paintings are exquisitely executed, with rich golden mists and clouds.

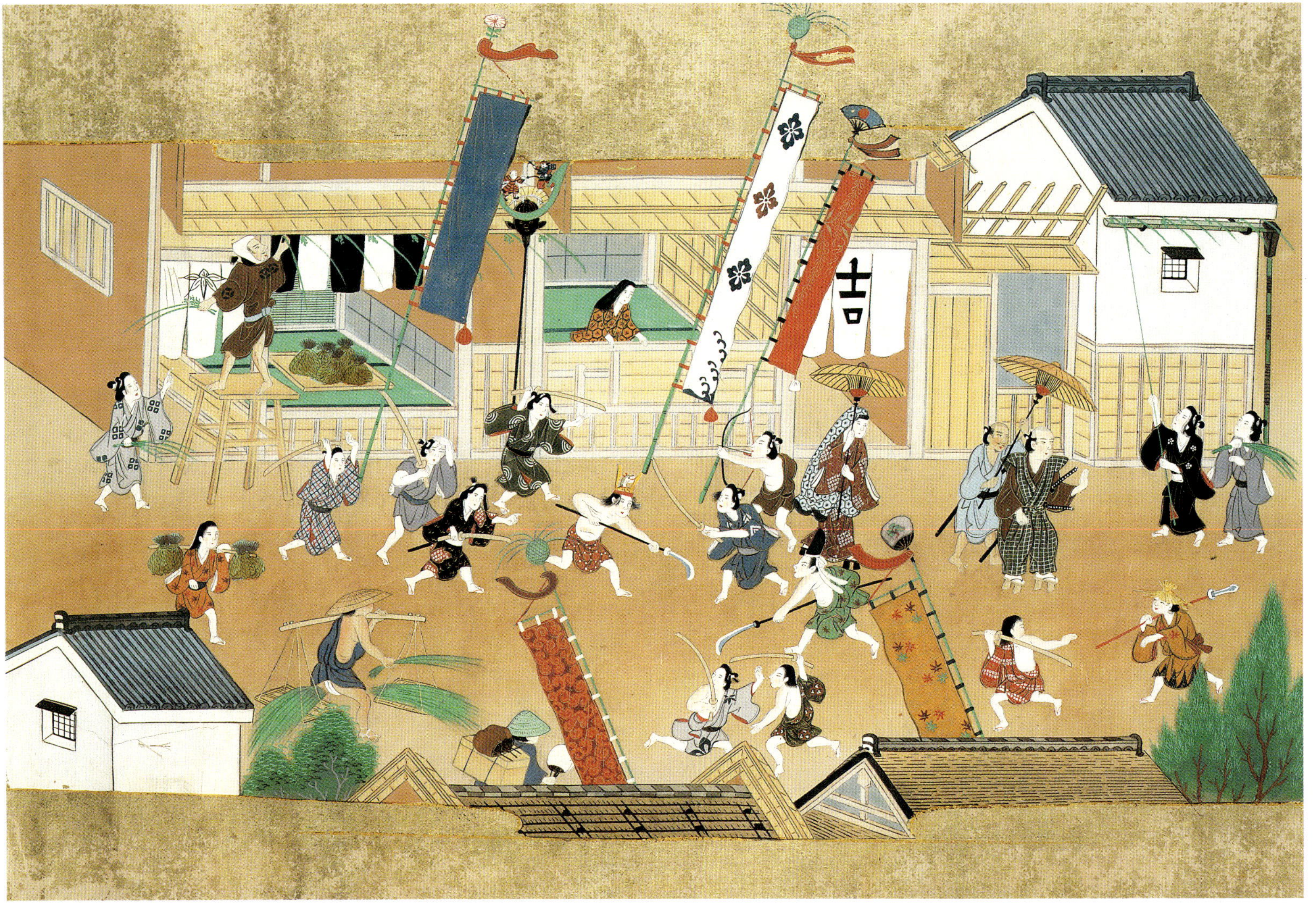

41.

41.

Jūnikagetsu Asobi Emaki

(Painted scrolls of the celebrations for the twelve months)

Anonymous

Middle of 17th century, Edo period

Two scrolls; ink, colors, and gold on paper

I: H 33 L 873; II: H 33 L 833

CBJ No. 1118 (27)

Nara-ehon-style paintings show some annual celebrations, mainly those based on festivals in each month. Text and some poems or selections of prose follow each scene accordingly. The paper is elegantly decorated with sprinkled gold dust and designs of flowers and grasses in gold paint. These paintings also provide valuable information on the customs and lives of common people in the Edo period.

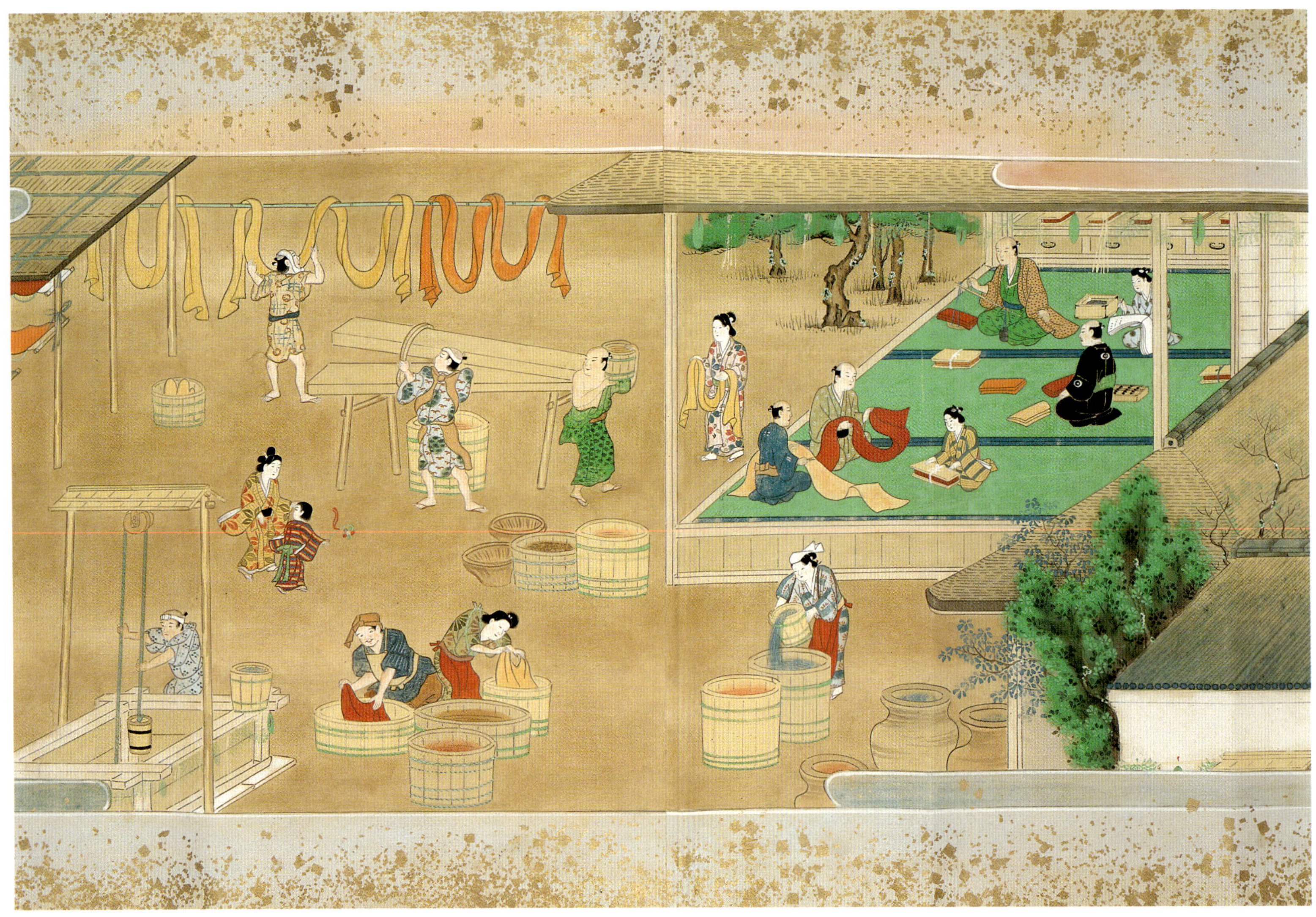

42.

42.

Chitose no Ubugi Emaki

(Painted scrolls of Chitose no Ubugi)

Anonymous

End of 17th century, Edo period

Two scrolls; ink, colors, silver, and gold on paper

I: H 33.5 L 668; II: H 33.5 L 662

CBJ No. 1139 (41)

Various activities that are largely connected with the making and selling of clothes for the New Year festivities are depicted here. Each process involved, such as cutting the silk cloth, bleaching, dyeing, embroidering, and hand-painting it and making braids, is portrayed in fine detail.

Even though there is no accompanying text, these scrolls nevertheless provide valuable material for the researcher of handcrafts and the artistry and techniques of cloth-making during the Edo period.

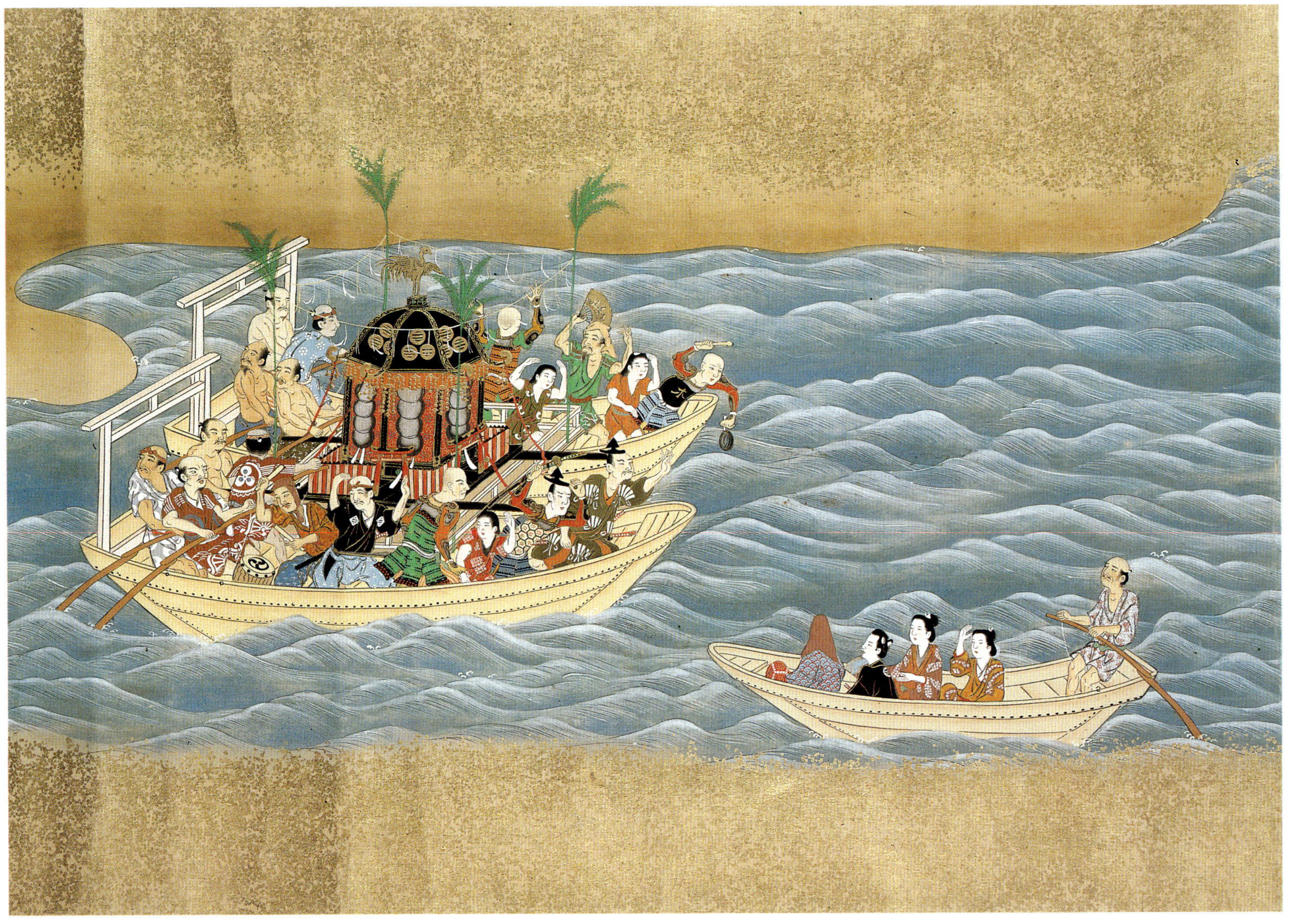

43.

43.

Sannōmatsuri Emaki

(Painted scroll of the Sannō Festival)

Anonymous

Middle of 17th century, Edo period

Two scrolls; ink, colors, and gold on paper

I: H 35 L 750; II: H 35 L 750

CBJ No. 1160 (17)

The paintings depict in full color the April festival procession of seven portable shrines *(mikoshi)*. The procession is first shown taking place in a street setting at Sakamoto, in Shiga prefecture, by Lake Biwa, while the second scroll portrays the shrines being carried across the lake in boats.

These paintings may have been produced as a pictorial record of the colorful Sannō Shrine Festival. There is no accompanying text.

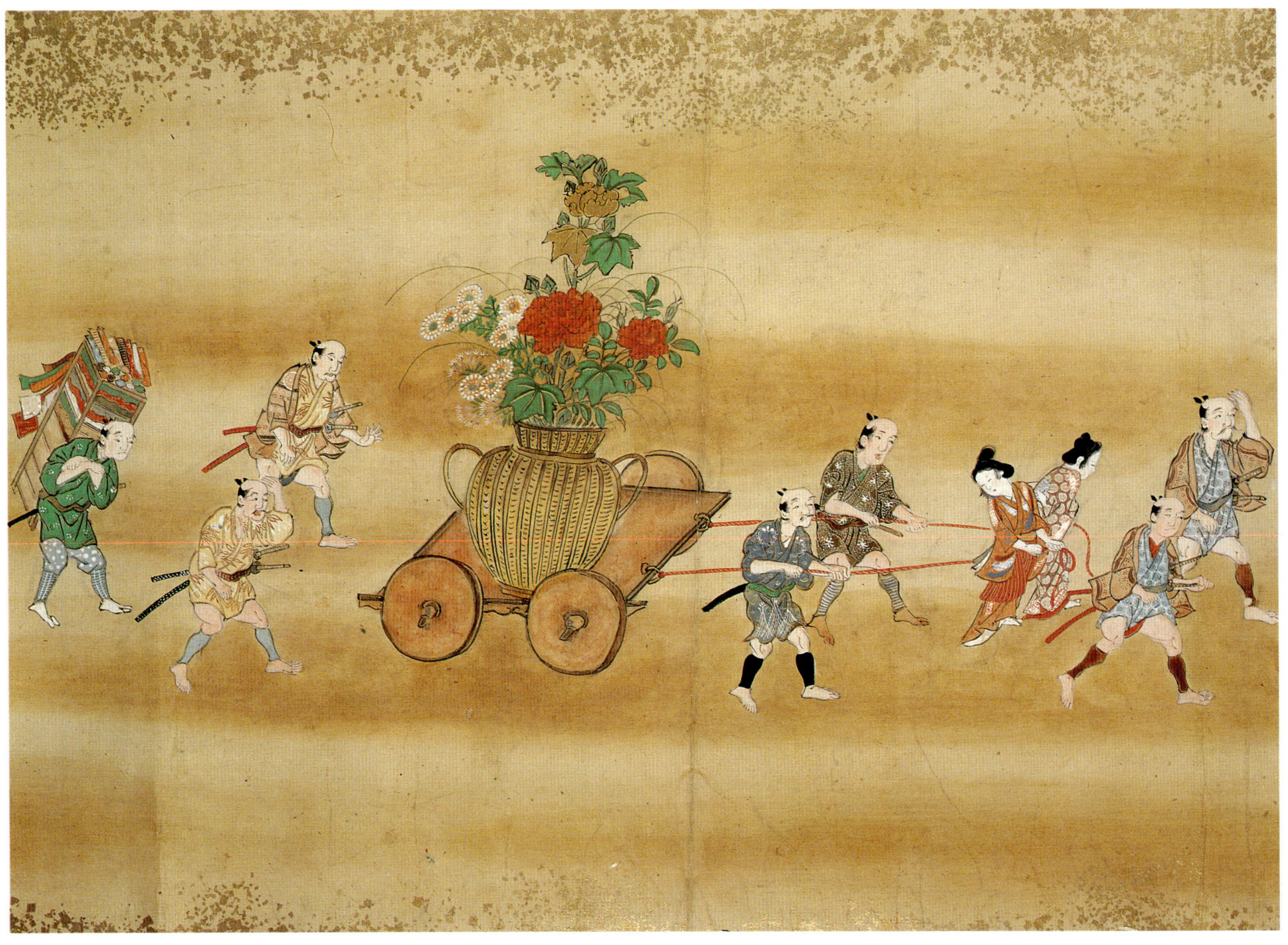

44.

44.

Sagamatsuri Emaki

(Painted scroll of the Saga Festival)

Anonymous

Middle of 17th century, Edo period

One scroll; ink, colors, silver, and gold on paper

H 31.7 L 657

CBJ No. 1142 (16)

Illustrated here is the festival procession of Atago Shrine as it descends from Atago Mountain to the Saga district of Kyoto. This annual rite still enjoys much popularity in Saga today. When this scroll was exhibited in Japan in 1988, the current Saga Festival committee expressed great delight and excitement in seeing it, since no other documental record of the procession from this early date exists. There is no accompanying text.

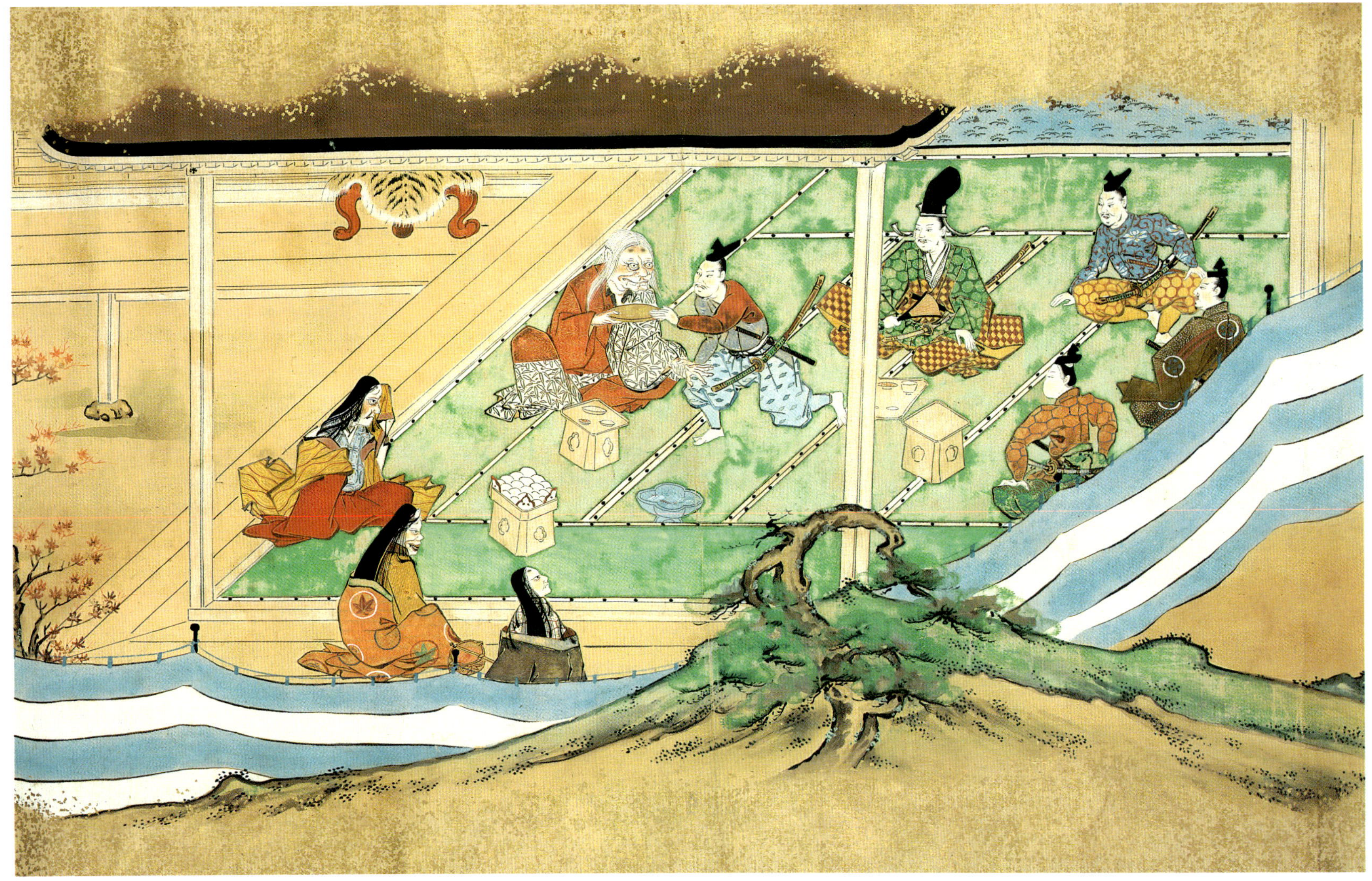

45.

45.

Momijiasobi Emaki

(Painted scrolls of festival processions)

Anonymous

End of 17th century, Edo period

Two scrolls; ink, colors, and gold on paper

I: H 32.7 L 648; II: H 32.7 L 747

CBJ No. 1115a, b (18)

Although the original title slips on the two scrolls say "Scrolls of the festival of maple viewing," the subjects are in fact quite different. The first scroll depicts a festival procession which is rather similar to that of the Saga Festival (cat. no. 44). The composition, however, is monotonous, and the figures appear rather stilted. The second scroll illustrates a devils' feast, followed by an ongoing battle with several warriors in which the devils are eventually defeated. Despite the contrast in subject matter, the two scrolls are similar in style and manner of execution, and may indeed have originated from the same studio.

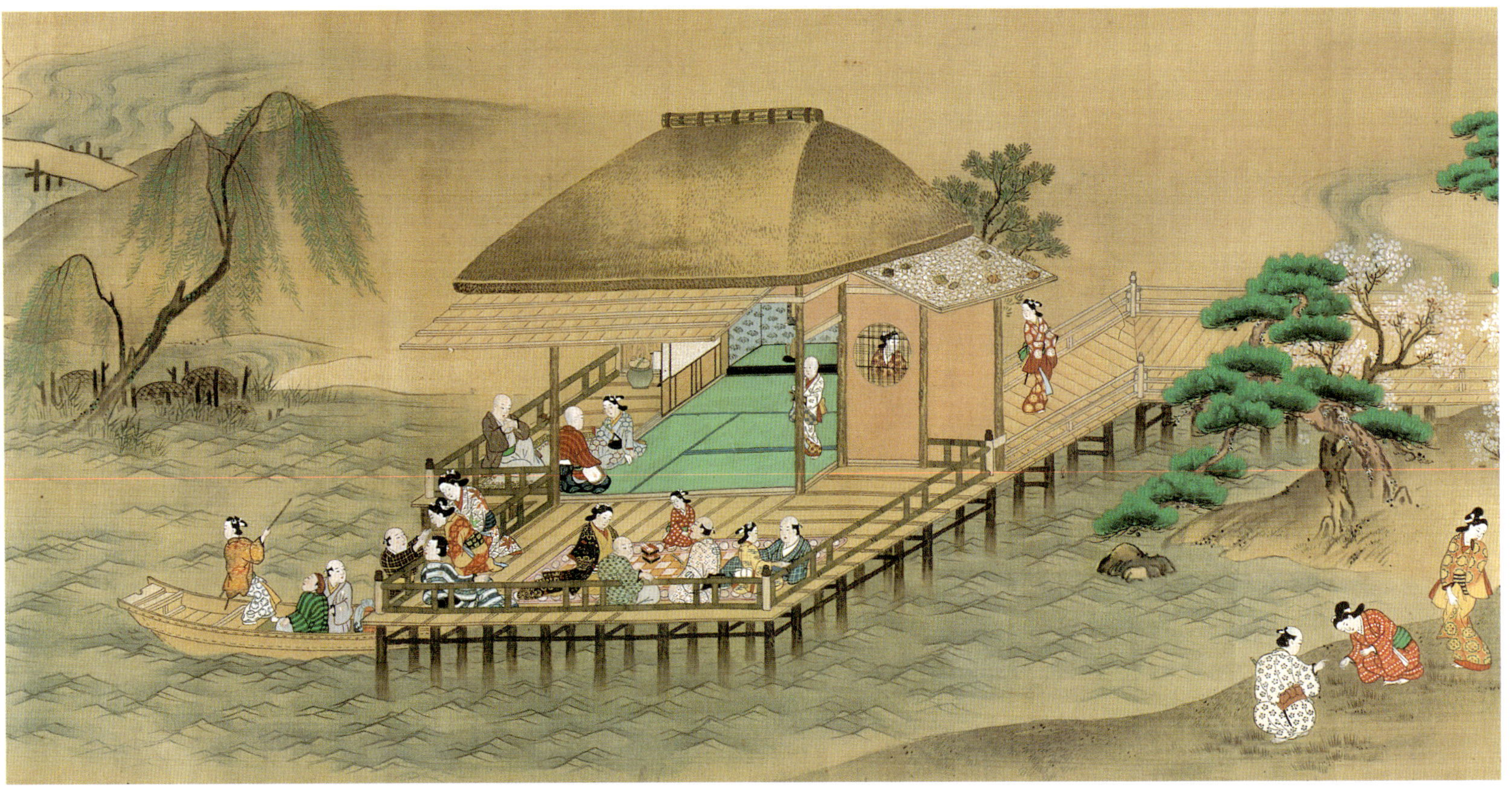

46.

46.

Shuihen Yūraku Zukan

(Painted scroll of leisurely activities by the waterside)

Miyagawa Chōshun (1682–1752)

Beginning of 18th century, Edo period

One scroll; ink, colors, silver, and gold on silk

H 33 L 209

CBJ No. 1123 (93)

Since the painting starts in an abrupt manner, this short scroll is most likely a portion from a scroll of an original *ukiyo-e* painting. It depicts in vivid detail various leisurely activities, such as dining at a luncheon party or drinking sake, taking place in the pleasure quarter by the waterside.

The artist Miyagawa Chōshun first studied under the Tosa school and later transferred to the *ukiyo-e* school, although his work is restricted to *ukiyo-e* painting rather than prints. He was particularly renowned for his paintings of beautiful women.

47.

Senmen Gajō

(An album of fan-shape paintings)

Anonymous

Beginning of 17th century, Edo period

One album; ink, colors, and gold on paper

H 31.2 W 61.5 (each frame)

CBJ No. 1003 (57)

The album contains five large and three small fan-shape paintings, all of which have fold marks, as if they were once actually mounted as fans. The first two paintings depict scenes of traditional Japanese court dance and music, and appear to form a pair. In the first painting, six *bugaku* dancers in customary T'ang-style Chinese dress are set against a gold background, which along the upper edge gives way to a red-brown hue. Of exquisite quality, the painting's style recalls some works by Tawaraya Sōtatsu (see cat. no. 5). In the companion piece, a varied decorative composition backed by gold clouds merges with a red-brown background along the upper edge. The style of the painting is again reminiscent of Sōtatsu's work, and both fans were probably products of one of the artistic fan shops with which Sōtatsu himself was associated.

The third painting depicts Chinese court life rendered in rich colors in the Tosa style. A puckered red pigment was used for the conventional clouds, and a thick white for the blossoms. Another on dark gray paper portrays a green-and-white phoenix in flight, with designs of paulownia interspersed with stylized clouds in gold outline. The fifth painting executed in the *hakubyō* style shows five hundred Buddhist disciples flying among the clouds.

The last fold in the album contains three smaller fans that seem to depict famous shrines and temples of the time in the Kyoto district, among them Kitano Shrine and Hōkōji Temple.

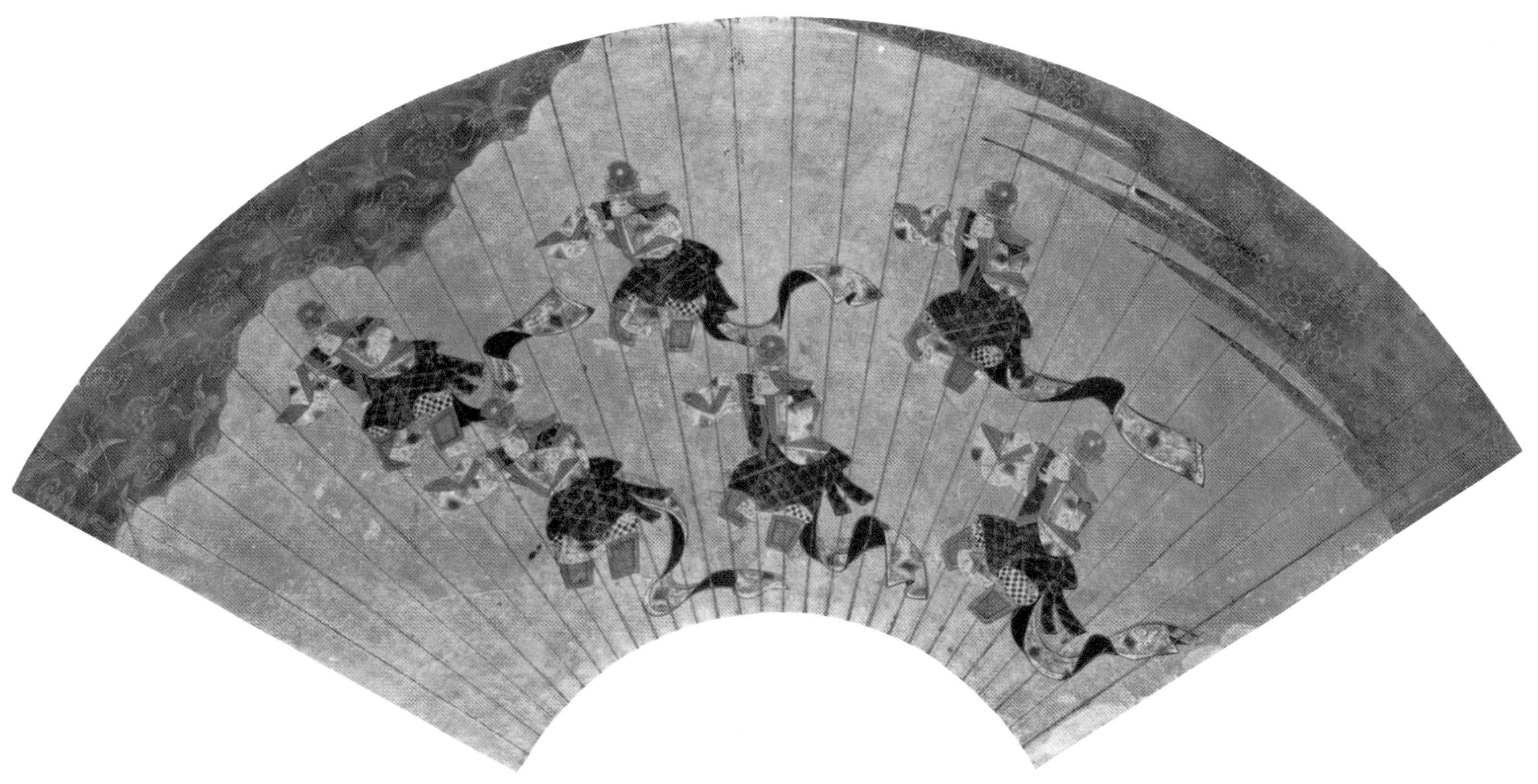

47.

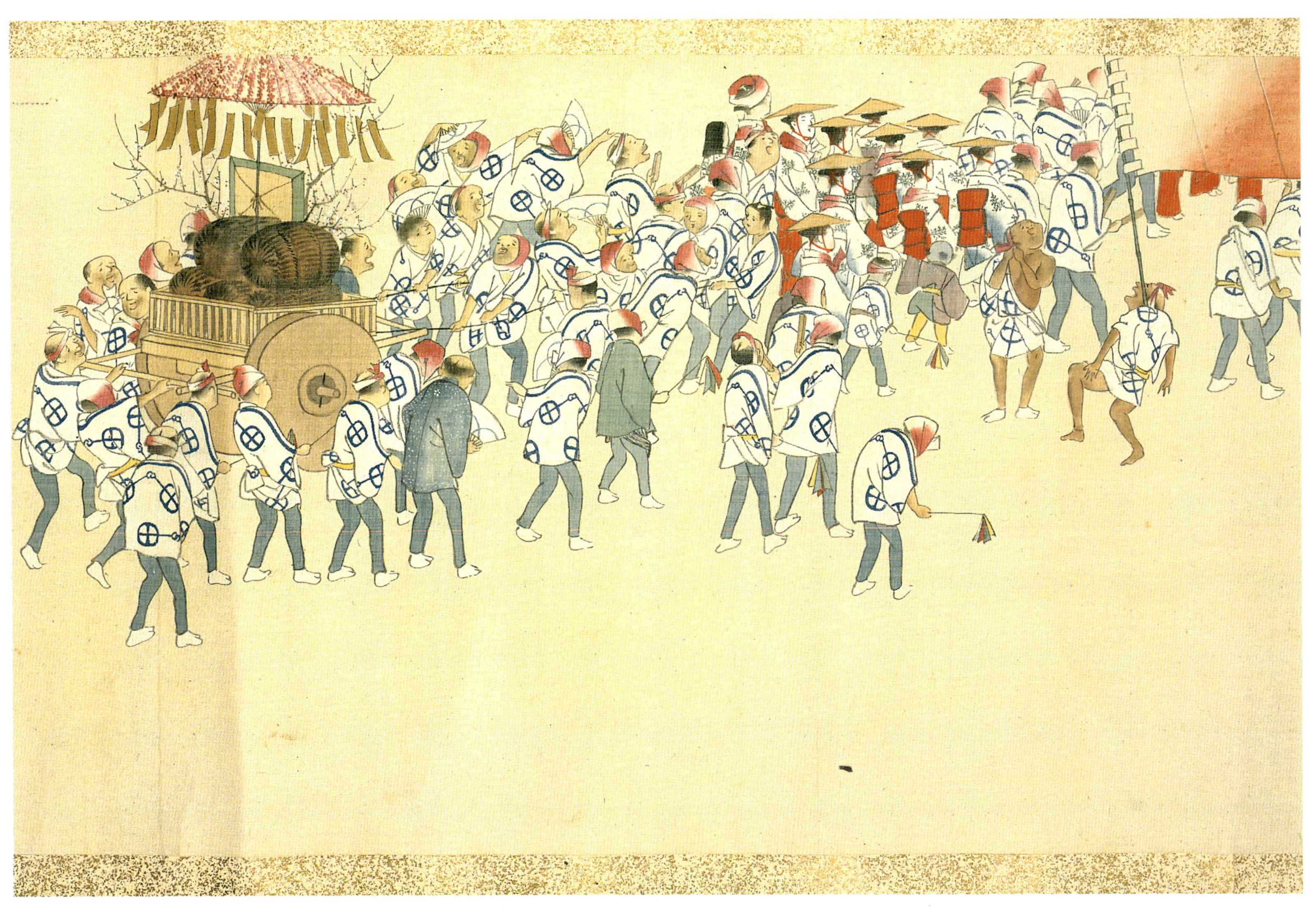

48. Celebrating the bountiful harvest of 1839

48.

I. Tempō Hachinen Kimin Kyūketsu Zukan
(Painted scroll of the 1837 famine)
II. Tempō Jūnen Hōnen Odori Zukan
(Painted scroll of the festival of good harvest of 1839)
Kino Yūbi, painter (1839–1933);
Kido Chitate, calligrapher (?–1845)
Middle of 19th century, Edo period
Two scrolls; ink, colors, silver, and gold on silk
I: H 33.5 L 705; II: H 33.5 L 1030
CBJ No. 1152 (111)

The first scroll contains realistic scenes of horror that occurred during the famine of 1837 in Kyoto, as well as the relief activities that followed. The second scroll captures the lively festival in Osaka that marked the first harvest after the famine of 1837 and shows people clad in fancy dress and dancing in the street with joyful exuberance.

According to Aiso Kazuhiro of the Osaka City Museum, Kino Yūbi, the artist of these scrolls, was not born until 1839, two years after the famine of 1837 (eighth year of Tempō), while Kido Chitate, the calligrapher, died in 1845, when Kino Yūbi was still less than seven years old.[16] Obviously they did not work together. Aiso suggests that the artist may have painted the scenes years afterwards from imagination, using Kido's text for his paintings.

It is interesting to note that the paintings are done on silk with the text written on paper which has been pasted onto the scrolls. The scrolls thus date from a period considerably later than that of the famine and harvest. Aiso adds that the Tempō era was marked by many famines and ensuing harvests. Subsequently this pair of scrolls was most likely commissioned to serve as a record of a particular event. The scrolls are therefore a valuable resource for research into the social state and the condition of life at that time.

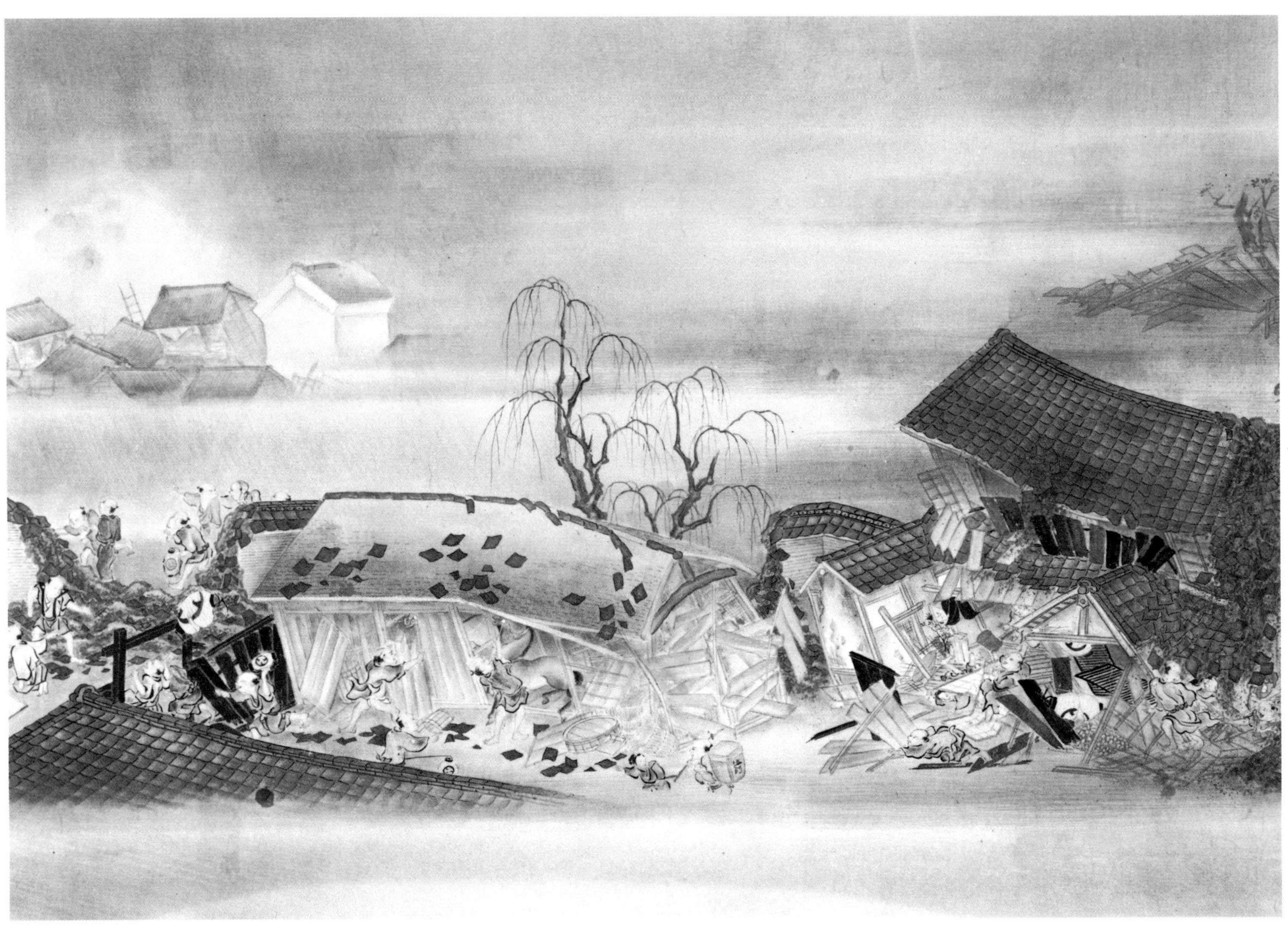

49.

49.

Ansei Daijishin Saika Zukan

(Painted scroll of the earthquake of 1855)

Anonymous

1855–56, Edo period

One scroll; ink, colors, and gold on paper

H 41.7 L 1036

CBJ No. 1150 (119)

The painting is a realistic depiction of the scenes of disaster that followed the earthquake of October 1855. The scroll begins with a colorful scene of maple trees and a peaceful night in Edo. Then, after a significant, long blank portion to symbolize the actual earthquake, the scenes of devastation follow: collapsed houses, broken roof slates, buildings destroyed by fire, human casualties, and other pitiful scenes, all detailed with the realism of a documental record. Although the subject matter is somewhat gruesome, the manner of painting possesses a subtle beauty and delicateness.

According to a memorandum written by Sir Chester Beatty in 1917, this scroll was painted at the request of Prince Konoe, one of the five great aristocratic families since the Kamakura period.

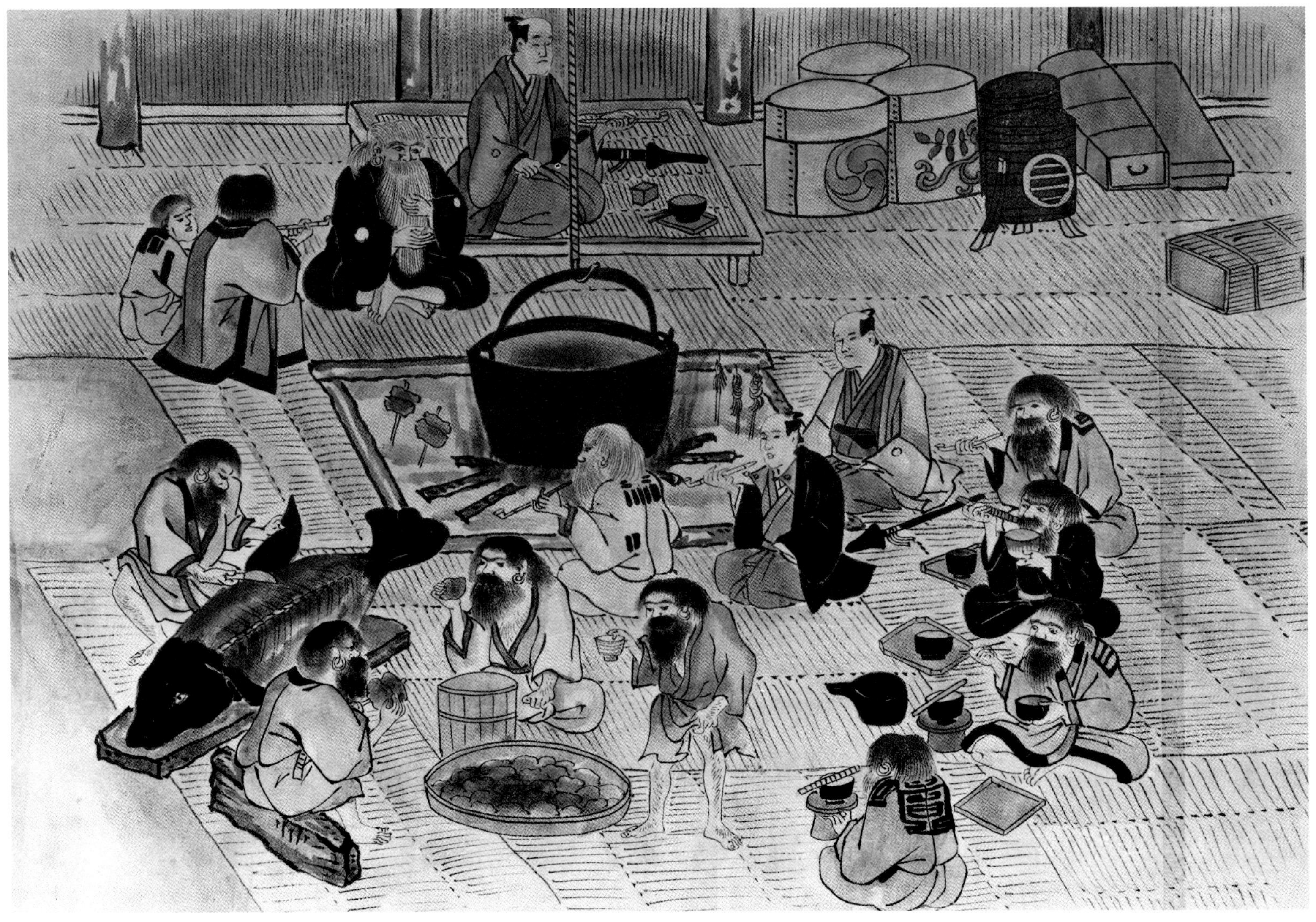

50.

50.

Ezo Kokkai Zukan

(Painted scroll of the life of the Ainu)

Anonymous

Middle of 19th century, Edo period

One scroll; ink and colors on paper

H 27.5 L 588

CBJ No. 1185 (116)

Fourteen paintings illustrate the life of the Ainu people, an exotic tribe that completely differed from the Japanese even though they lived in Hokkido, a northern island off the mainland. These works emphasize in particular the relationship between the Ainu and the native Japanese. A rare copy of an original Ainu work, the scroll is certainly valuable research material for ethnologists.

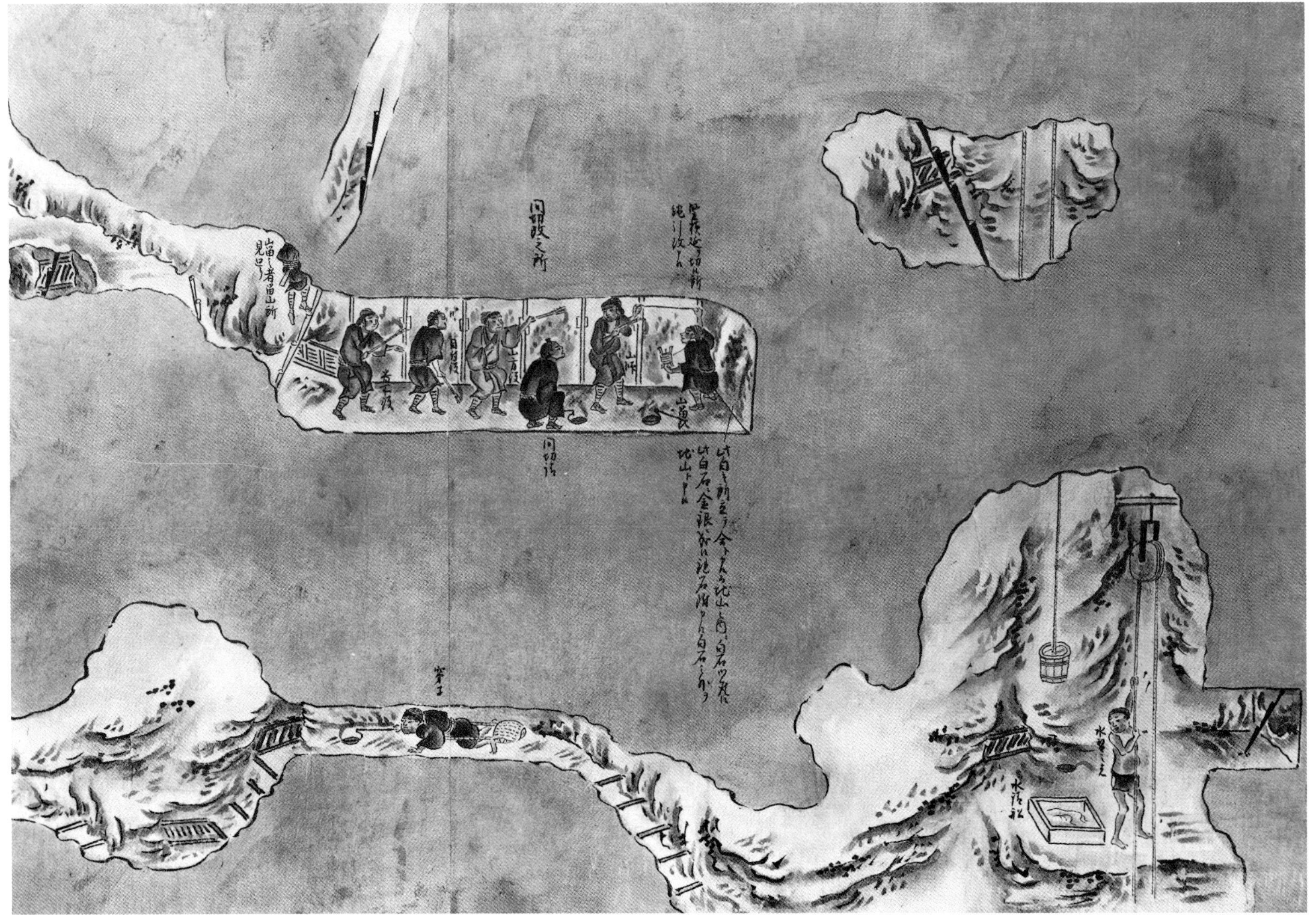

51.

51.

Sadokinzan Zukan

(Painted scrolls of the gold mine in the Sado district)

Anonymous

19th century, Edo period

Three scrolls; ink and light colors on paper

I: H 32 L 1224; II: H 32 L 814;

III: H 32 L 988

CBJ No. 1134 (117)

Paintings in ink and light colors present in meticulous detail the various stages involved in mining and minting gold on Sado Island. It was declared a special territory under the direct control of the shogunate when gold was discovered there around 1600.

As a mining engineer himself, Sir Chester Beatty was very pleased when he purchased this unique set of scrolls in 1953 from a Dr. Gowland, who had spent years in Japan during the early Meiji era as chief officer of the Mint Bureau in Tokyo.

The scrolls are extremely valuable as a technical record of gold mining of the time, documenting in particular the process of working on the mines in tunnels.

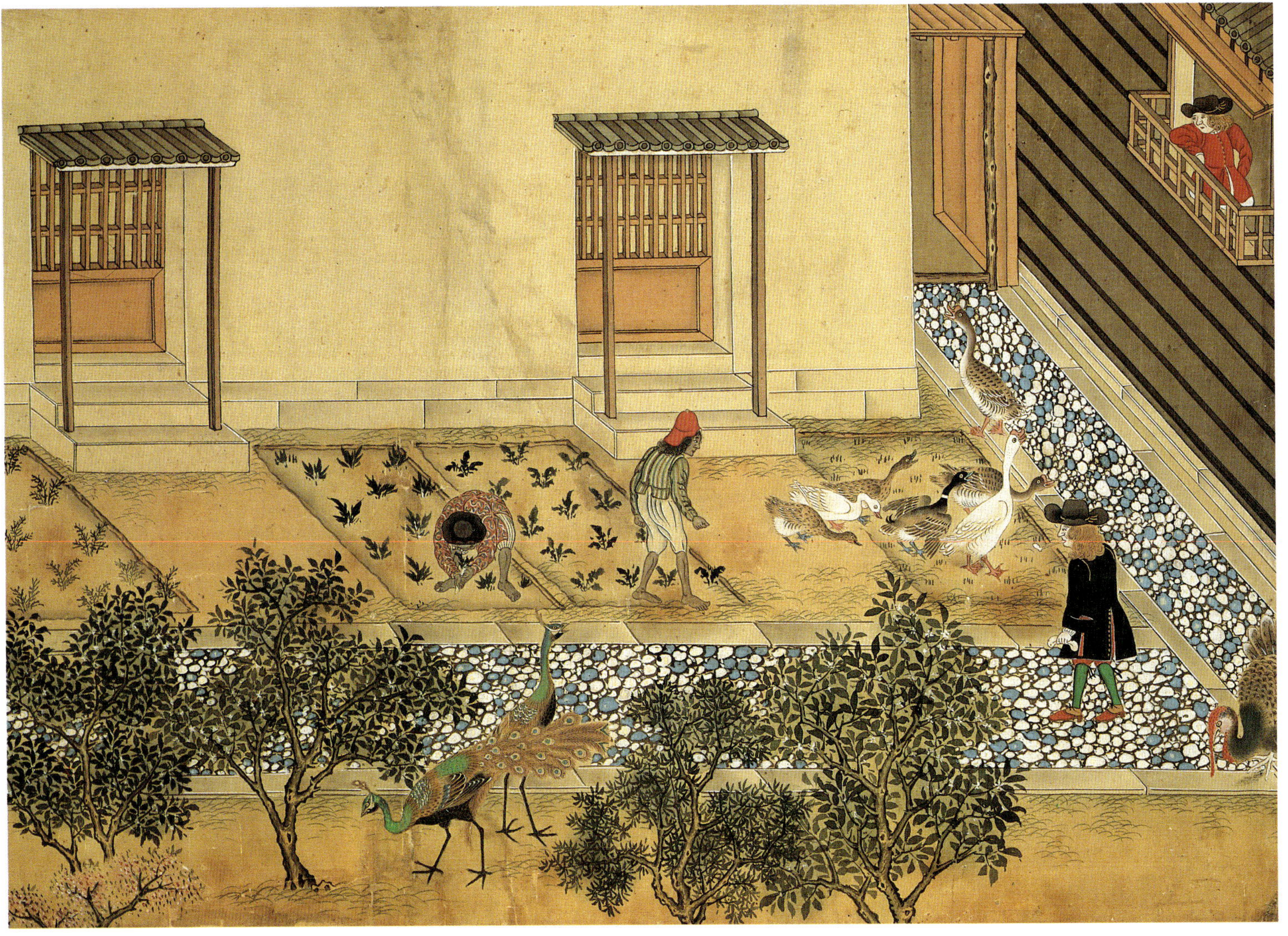

52.

52.

Nagasaki Dejima Rankan no Zu

(Paintings of the Dutch mansions in Nagasaki)

Anonymous

18th century, Edo period

Two portions from a painted scroll; ink, colors, and gold on silk

I: H 33 L 89.5; II: H 33 L 123.5

CBJ No. 1131 (98)

Shown here is the everyday life of the Dutch merchants in their special living and trading quarters on the island of Dejima in Nagasaki. These paintings, in rich colors on silk, are in the style of the Nagasaki school.

A scroll of the same subject on paper and attributed to Watanabe Shūkoku (1639–1707) is known to exist. While the Chester Beatty work is very similar in composition, unfortunately it is only two sections and not a complete scroll.

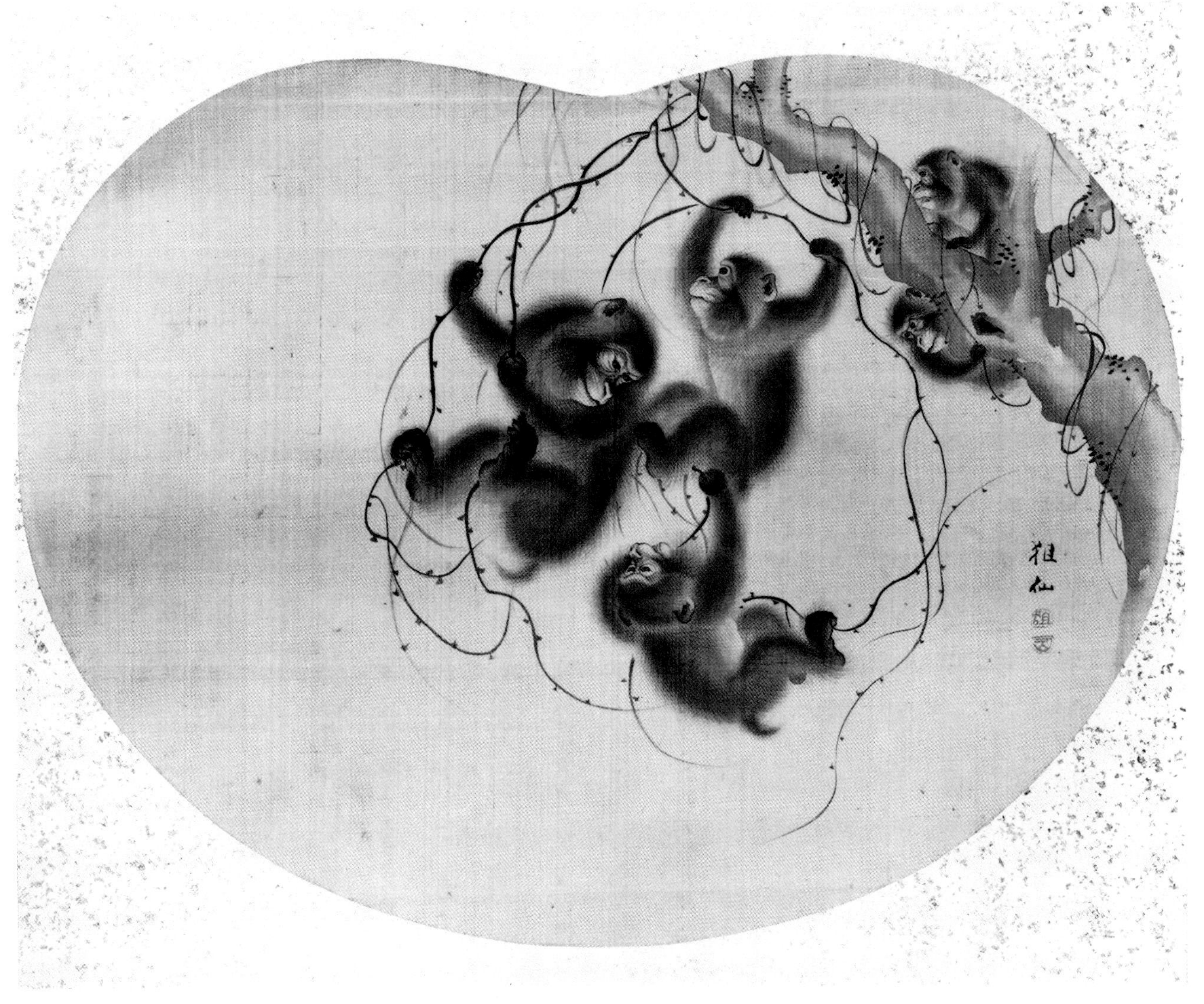

53.

53.

Enkō Zujō

(Painted album of monkeys)

Mori Sosen (1747–1821)

Beginning of 19th century, Edo period

One album; ink and light colors on silk

H 33.4 W 38

CBJ No. 1042 (107)

This concertina-style album contains eight paintings of monkeys, each rendered in light colors on fan-shape silk. The accurate depictions of the animals' delicate facial expressions and movements reveal a careful study of detail. All the paintings are signed and sealed individually by Mori Sosen, renowned for his paintings of animals and of monkeys in particular. It is said that he spent much of his time in the mountains observing monkeys and their behavior.

The animals are set against an elegant background of natural flora and fauna, including an aged tree, ivy, grasses with insects, and tree branches, as well as a waterfall and the moon above.

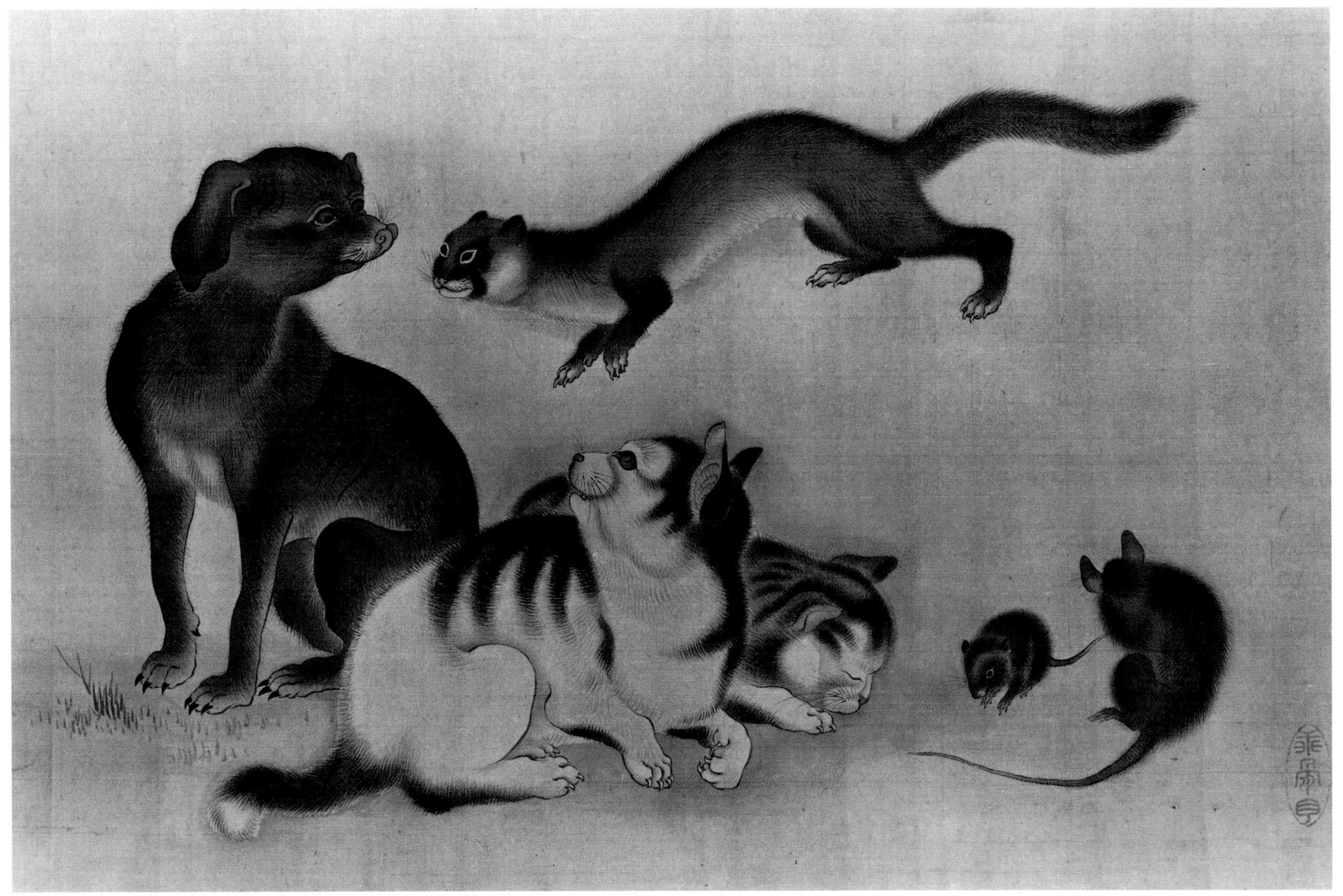

54.

54.

Dōbutsu Zukan

(Painted scrolls of animals)

Attributed to Mori Sosen (1747–1821)

Beginning of 19th century, Edo period

Two scrolls; ink and colors on silk

I: H 38.5 L 407; II: H 38.5 L 423

CBJ No. 1116 (108)

The scrolls reveal a series of animals painted in various colors on fine silk. Although executed in minute and delicate detail, the paintings seem to lack a certain strength.

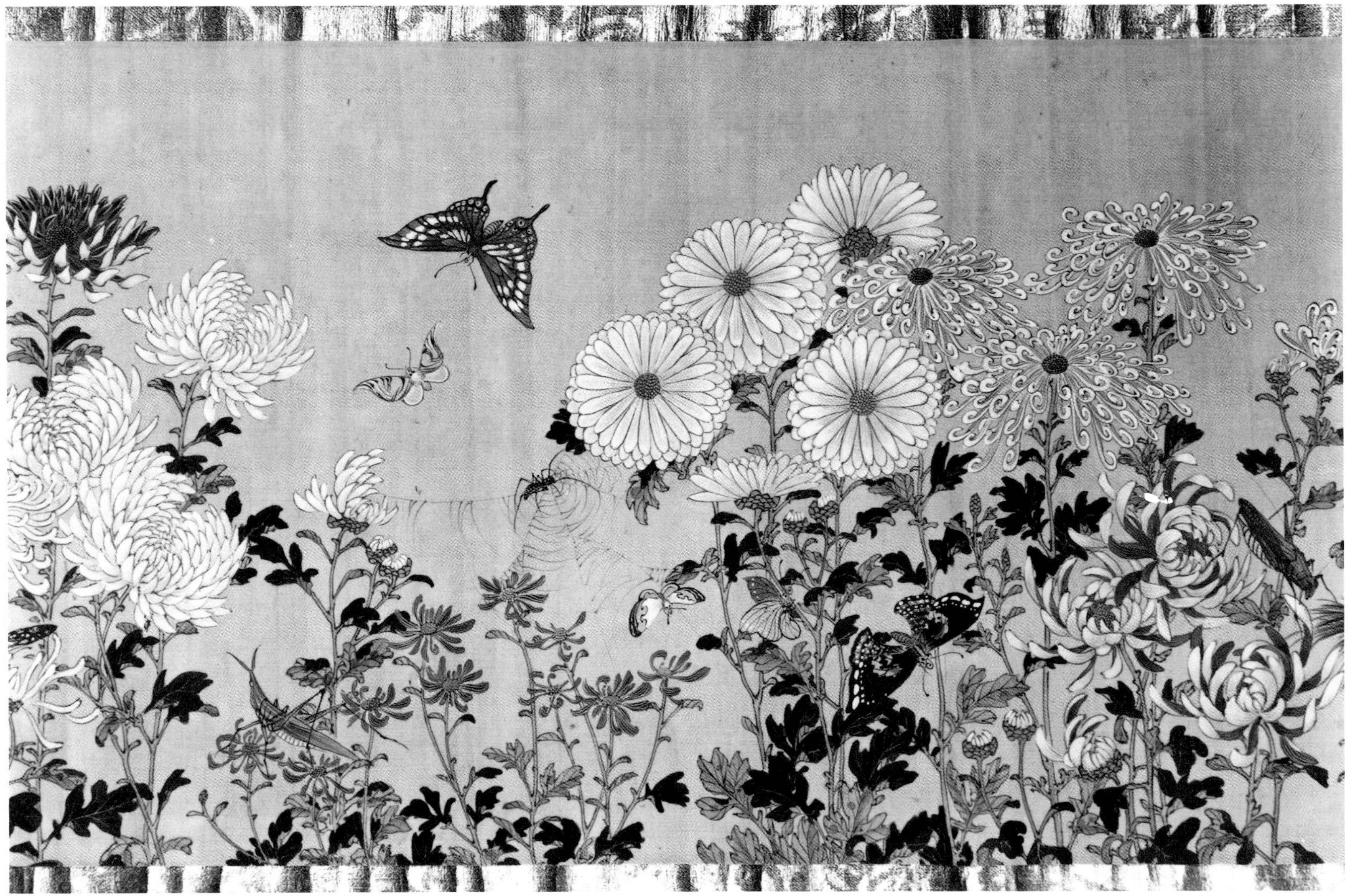

55.

55.

Chōgiku Zukan

(Painted scroll of butterflies and chrysanthemums)

Anonymous

Middle of 19th century, Edo period

One scroll; ink, colors, silver, and gold on silk

H 26 L 283

CBJ No. 1144 (110)

Chrysanthemums of different species are delicately painted in vivid hues on silk, with various kinds of colorful butterflies fluttering gracefully among the flowers. Realistic in execution, the paintings convey the elegant beauty of nature.

The anonymous artist was undoubtedly influenced by the style of Chinese flower painting practiced in the eighteenth and nineteenth centuries. The paintings are certainly of interest to naturalists.

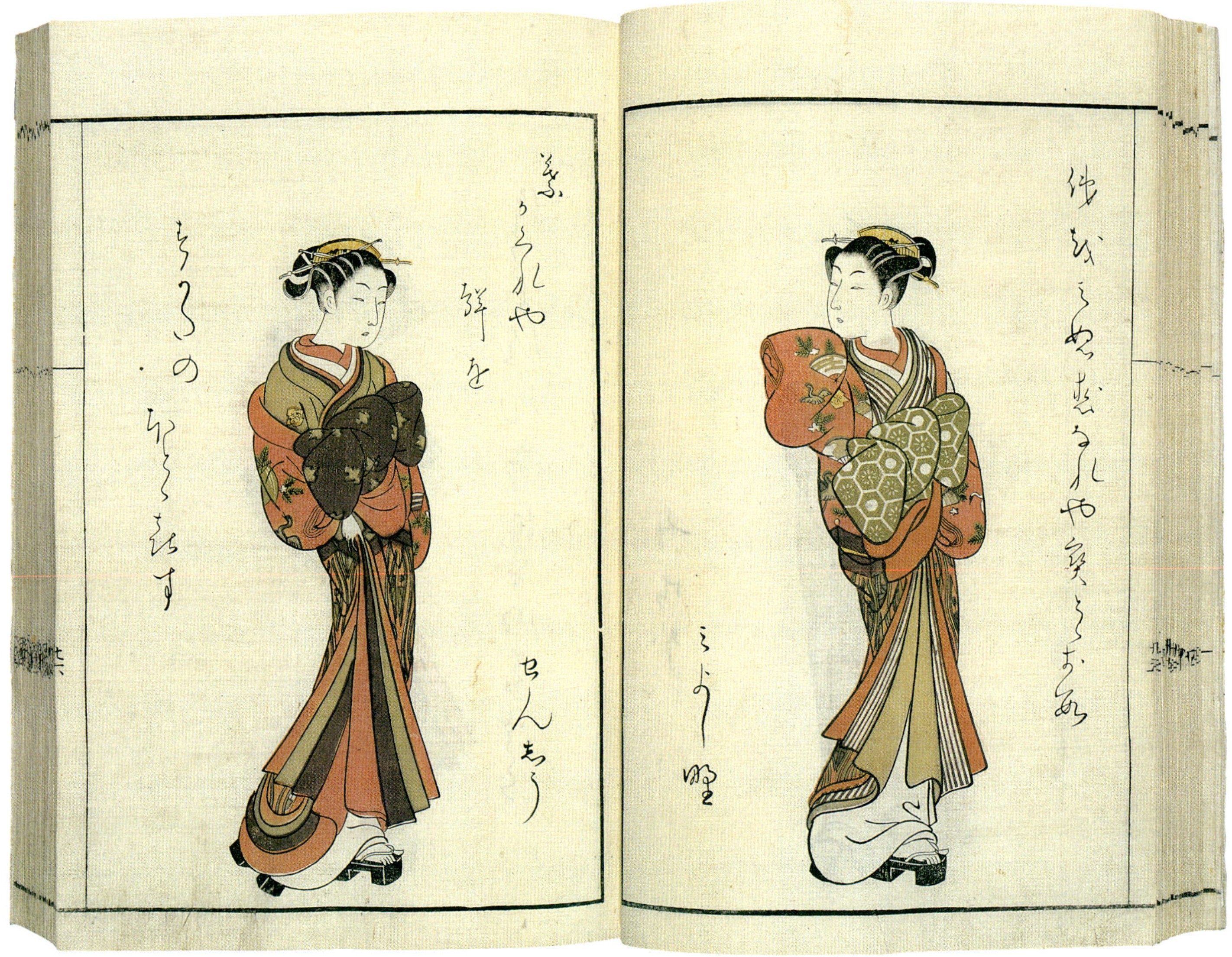

56.

56.

Seirō Bijin Awase

(A contest among the beautiful women of the Green House, Yoshiwara)

Suzuki Harunobu (1724–1770)

1770, Edo period

One volume; printed in ink and colors on paper

H 25.5 W 18

CBJ No. 1653 (136)

This is undoubtedly Harunobu's most famous and influential work. The original five volumes are bound together in one thick book and are classified according to the four seasons: spring, summer (two volumes), autumn, and winter. They comprise a collection of 166 color portraits of courtesans, each accompanied by the woman's name and a *hokku* poem (of 5-7-5 syllable lines).

While it is difficult to gauge accurately the influence of this fine early example of color images in printed books, there is little doubt that with its soft delicate greens against a gray background, the intricate details of the courtesans' kimonos, and of course the varied poses and activities of the subjects, the collection of illustrations served as a source of inspiration for Harunobu's contemporaries. Dated 1770, the Chester Beatty work seems to be one of the earliest printed copies of the first edition.

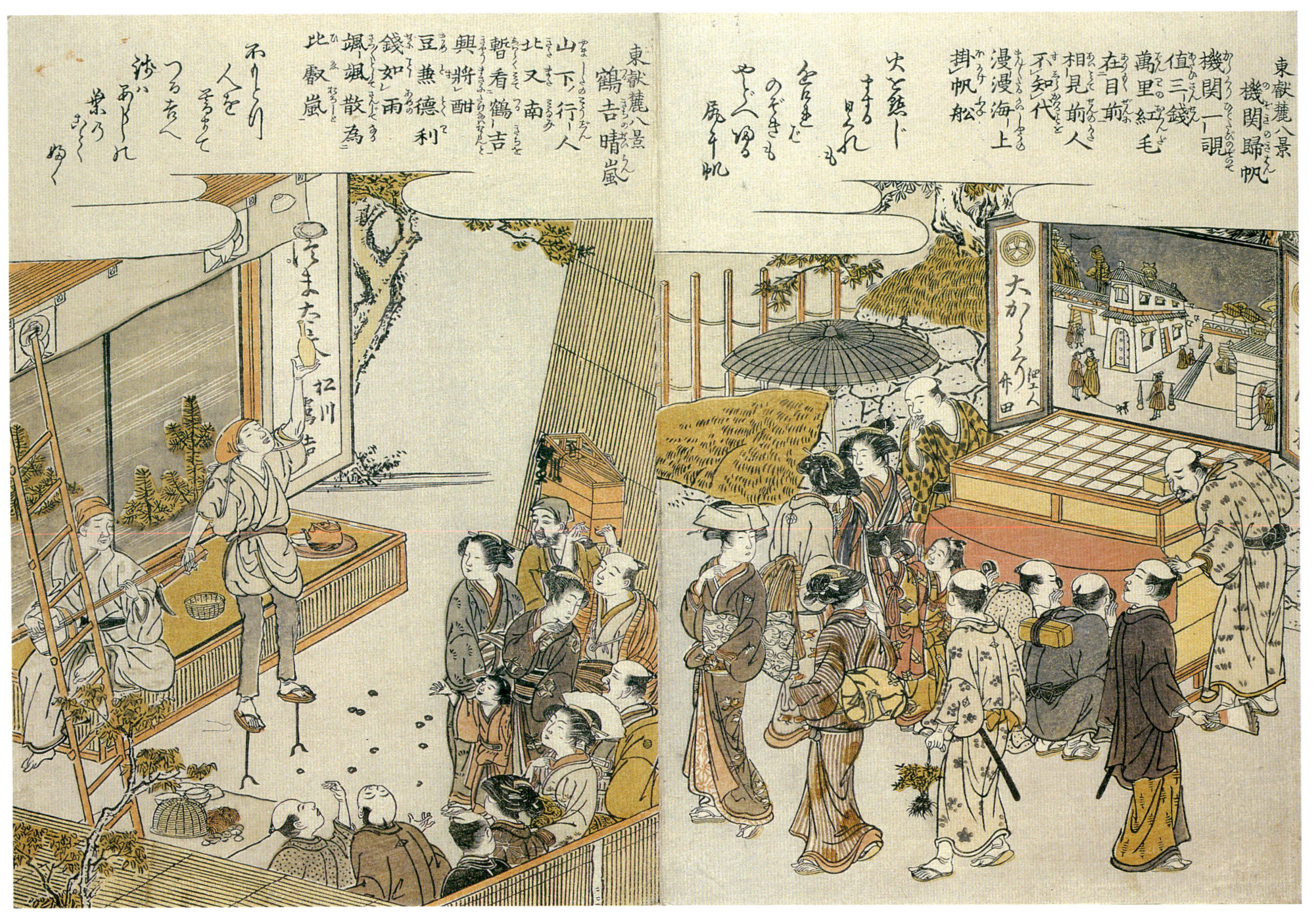
東叡麓八景
機関帰帆
機関一覗値三銭
萬里紅毛在目前
相見前人不知代
漫漫海上掛帆船
大からくり
細工人
竹田
東叡麓八景
鶴吉晴嵐
山下行人北又南
暫看鶴吉興将酣
豆蕪徳利銭如雨
颯颯散為比叡嵐
松川
鶴吉

57.

57.

Tōeizan Fumoto Hakkei

(Eight views of Tōeizan)

Attributed to Isoda Koryūsai (fl. ca. 1764–88)

Middle of 18th century, Edo period

One volume; printed in ink and colors on paper

H 24.7 W 18.5

CBJ No. 1680 (139)

Eight single page illustrations depict street scenes around Kaneiji Temple at Tōeizan in Edo. The artist is anonymous, but according to many specialists, he may have been Isoda Koryūsai. Each illustration is headed with an appropriate *kyōka,* a humorous poem of 5-7-5-7-7 syllables. The scenes represent the lively customs of the townsfolk of Edo of the time.

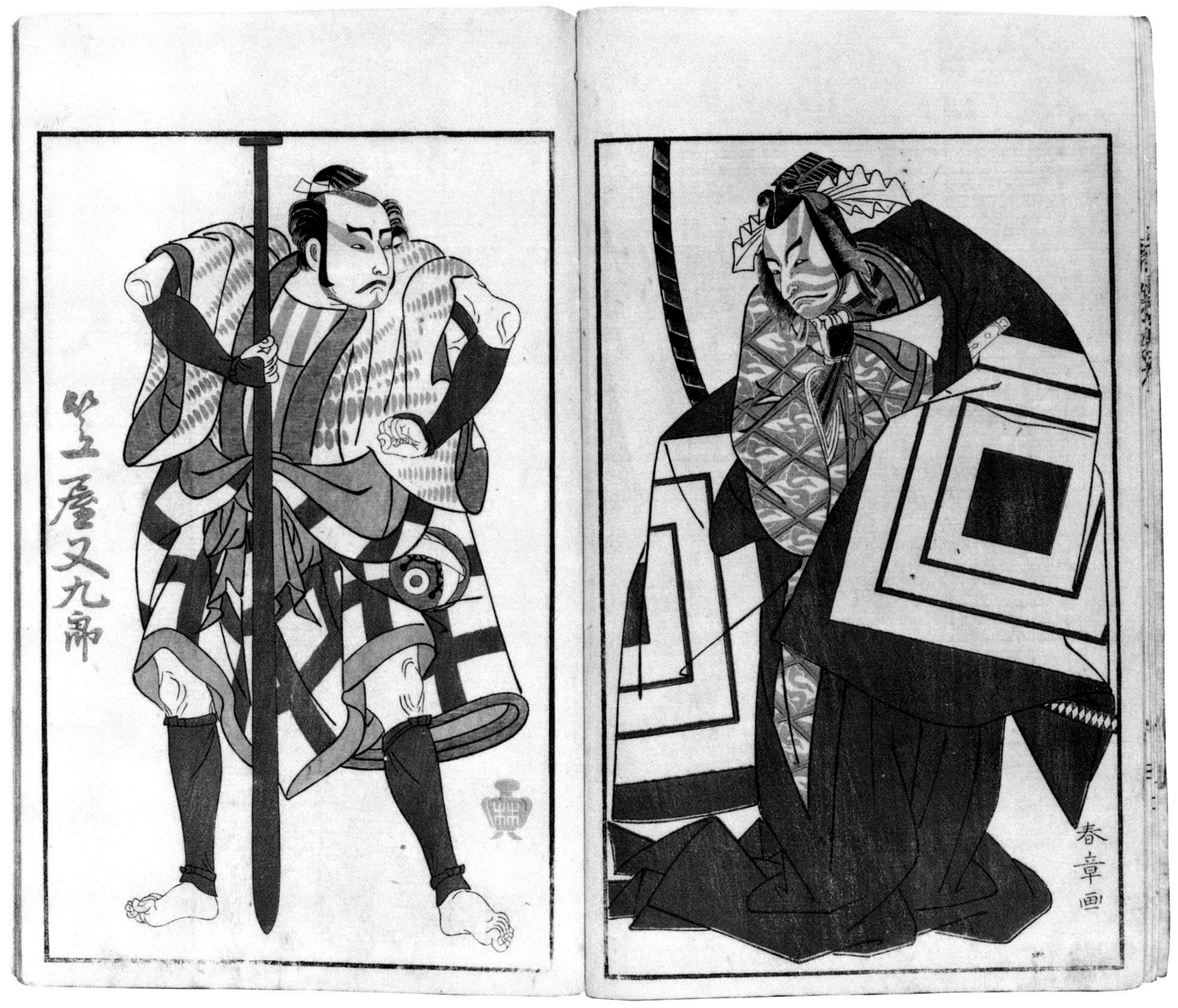

58.

58.

Ehon Butai no Ōgi

(Illustrated book of Kabuki stage fans)

Katsukawa Shunshō (1726–1792) and Ippitsusai Bunchō (fl. ca. 1765–1792)

1770, Edo period

Three volumes; printed in ink and colors on paper

H 28.3 W 18.2 (each)

CBJ No. 1644 (137)

Katsukawa Shunshō's first published work, produced in collaboration with Ippitsusai Bunchō, did not appear until 1770. This collection of color portraits of actors painted on fans was Shunshō's first attempt at a subject that was to make his reputation. His contribution to this already well-known *ukiyo-e* theme was his realistic treatment of the subjects and removing the actors from the roles that they played.

This set of volumes is an early printed copy of the first edition.

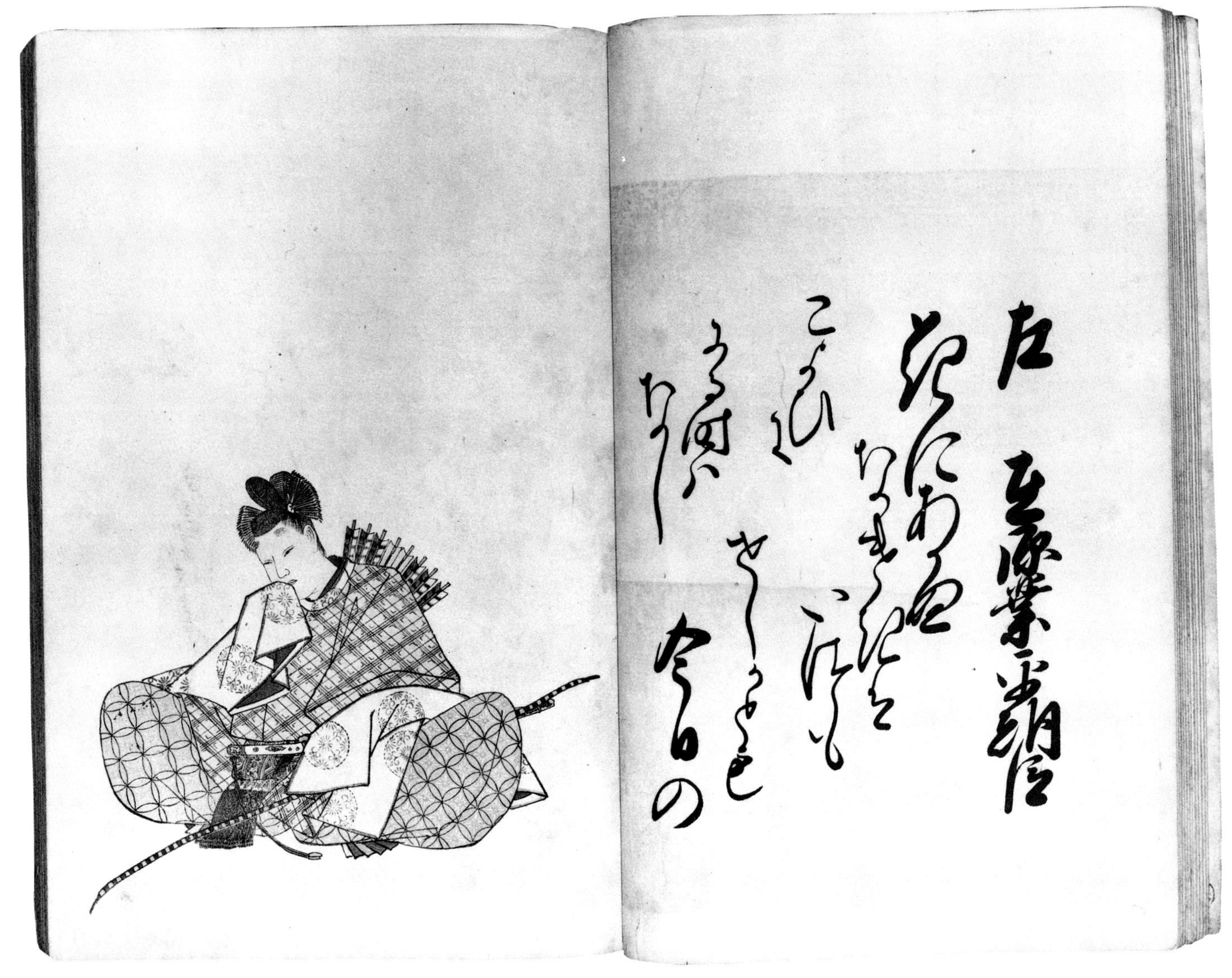

59.

59.
Sanjūrokkasen
(The Thirty-six Immortals of Japanese Poetry)
Katsukawa Shunshō (1726–1792)
1789, Edo period
One volume; printed in ink and colors on paper
H 29.4 W 21
CBJ No. 1649 (142)

Seven pages of preface by Sayama Chikayuki, who probably assembled this volume, are followed by a portrait of Dainagon Kintō, the compiler of this anthology. Shunshō's portraits of the poets are placed individually on separate pages with a corresponding poem on the reverse side. The artist's fine skill in portraiture is well represented in this work.

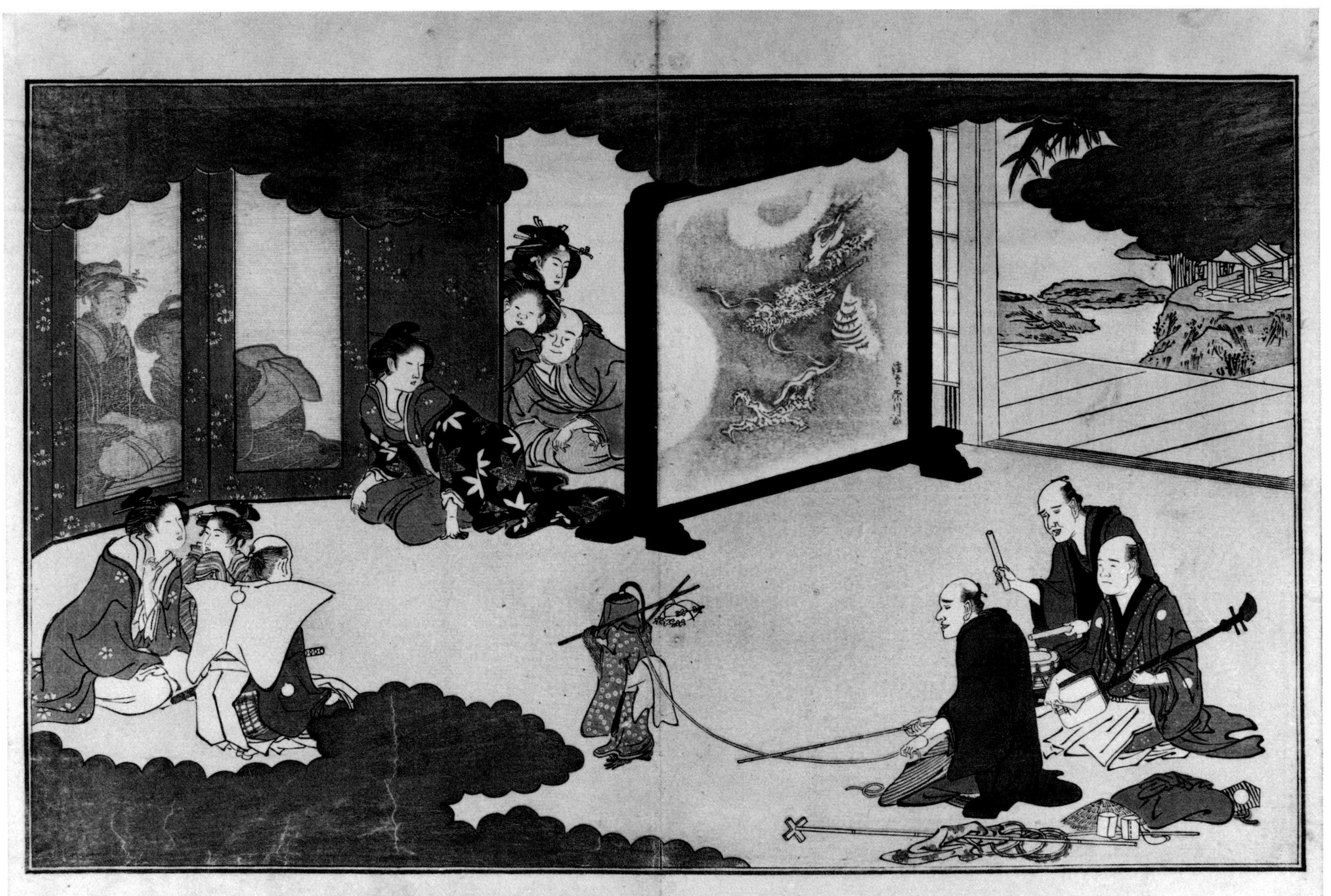

60.

60.

Wakaebisu

(Ebisu and the New Year Festival)

Kitagawa Utamaro (1754–1806)

1792, Edo period

One album; printed in ink, colors, silver, and gold on paper

H 25.5 W 18.9

CBJ No. 1670 (145)

An anthology of *kyōka* (humorous poems) on the theme of the New Year season is enlivened with four double-page illustrations in full color and gold and silver gaufrage. Utamaro's skill as an artist can be seen in particular in the depiction of the figures placed behind the folding screens and in the rendering of the painted screens (in the form of Tsuitate). The rich gold cloud patterns are typical of the Tosa style. This printed album constitutes one of the most precious works by Utamaro.

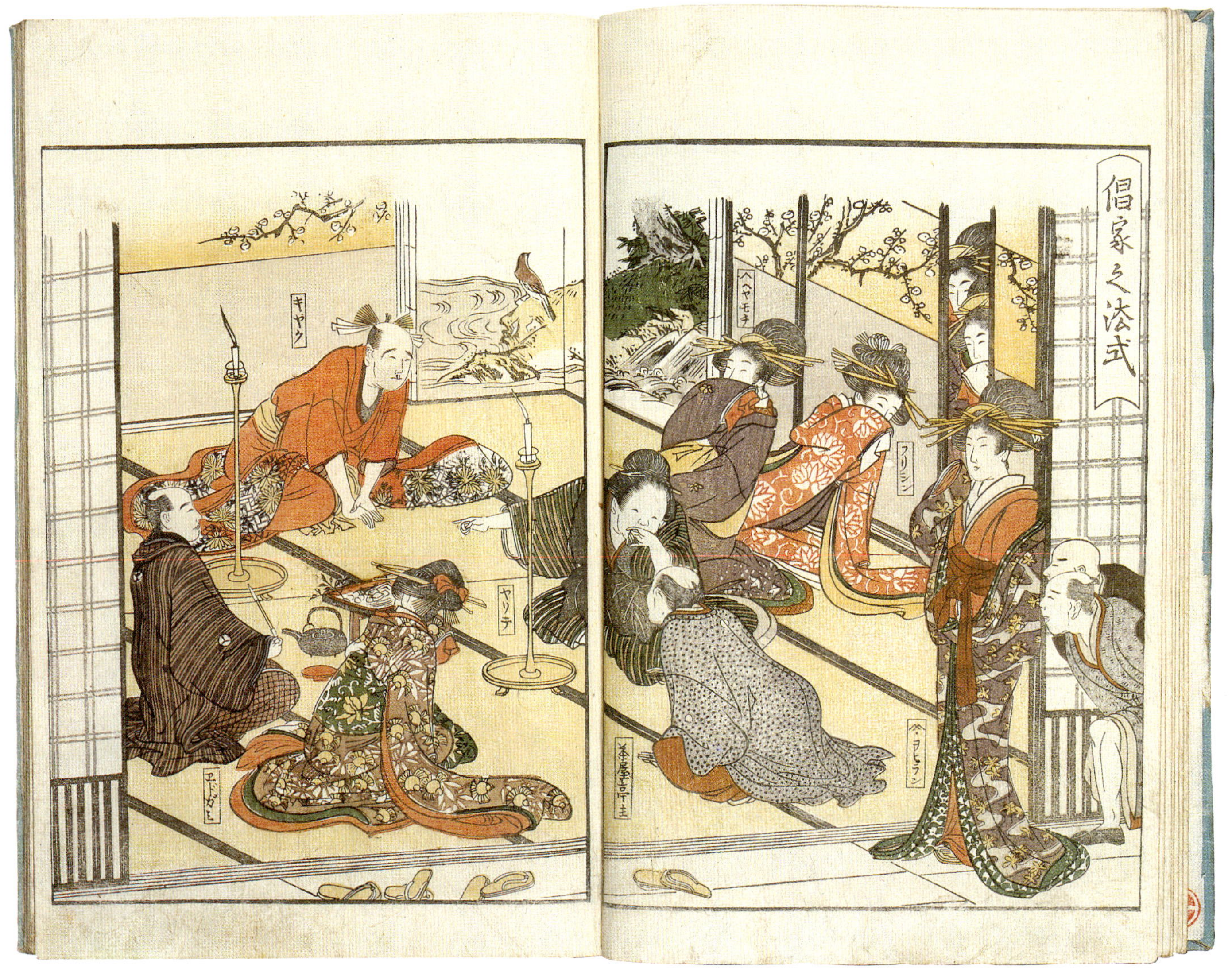

61.

61.

Seirō Ehon Nenjū Gyōji

(Annual activities of the Green House)

Kitagawa Utamaro (1754–1806)

1804, Edo period

Two volumes; printed in ink and colors on paper

H 22.5 W 15.9 (each)

CBJ No. 1684 (162)

With a text by Jippensha Ikku, this picture book describes annual activities in the pleasure quarters. The illustrations—volume 1 contains ten double-page illustrations, and volume 2 has nine—were done by Utamaro with the assistance of his pupils Kikumaro, Hidemaro, and Takemaro. This is one of the early printed copies of the first edition.

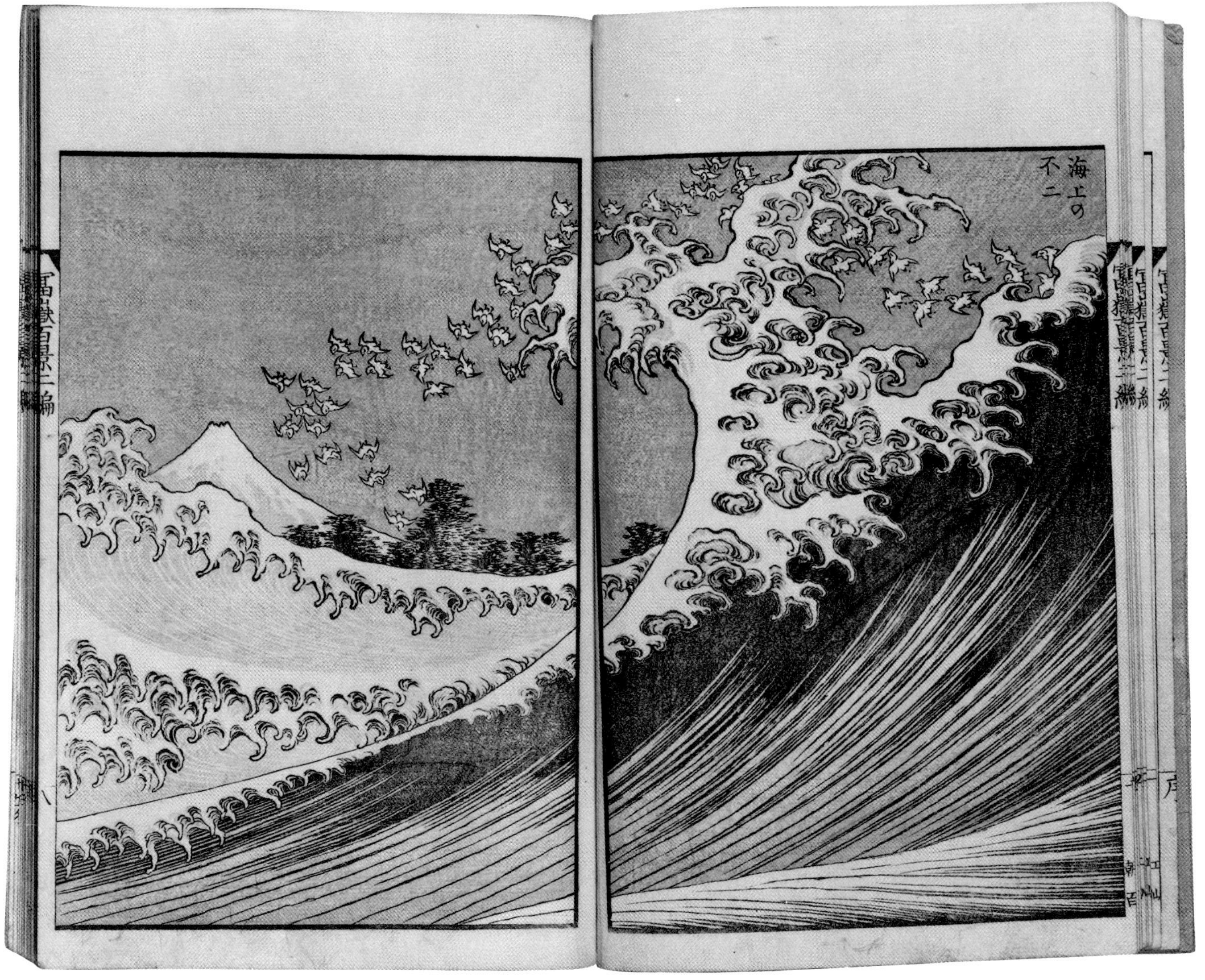

62.

62.

Fugaku Hyakkei

(One hundred views of Mount Fuji)

Katsushika Hokusai (1760–1849)

1834–35, Edo period

Three volumes; printed in ink

H 22.5 W 15.6 (each)

CBJ No. 1614 (179)

This is one of Hokusai's finest works. Volumes 1 and 2 are first editions, known as the falcon feather edition, while volume 3 was printed a year later by Eirakuya in Nagoya. The covers of the first edition are salmon pink with embossed designs of the eight views of Ōmi. On the title slip a stylized falcon's feather is printed in blue, a feature which may have derived from the traditional Japanese saying, "First is Fuji; second, the falcon; and third, the eggplant."

All the illustrations printed throughout the volumes are in black and white only, the highly skilled use of ink giving the pictures an impressive and elegant quality. While some are realistic sketches of Mount Fuji, many are much more stylized in effect. Some designs are based on traditional Japanese stories and legends centering around this famous mountain.

This set of volumes represents one of the most important of Hokusai's works and demonstrates the magnificent skill inherent in his designs.

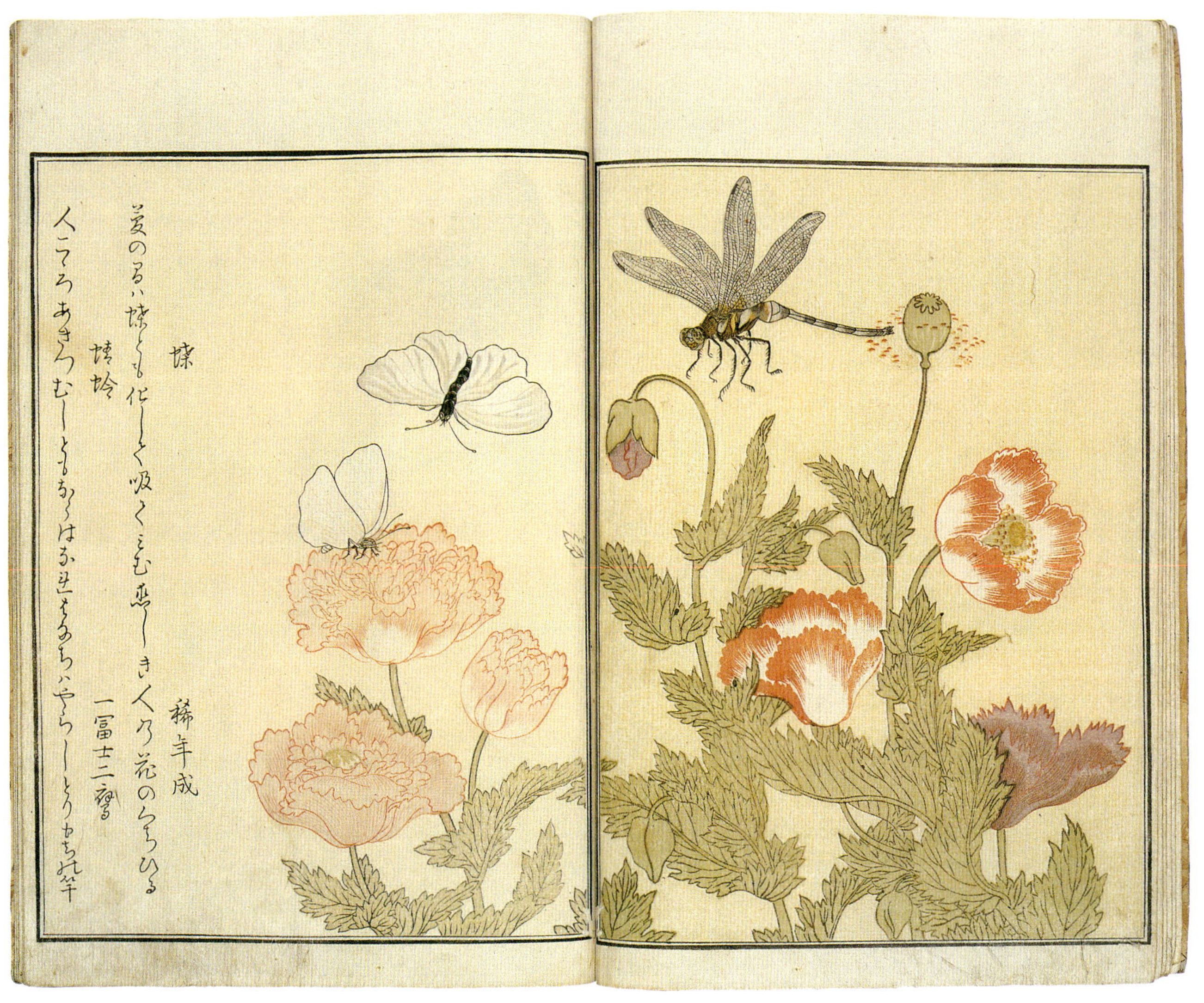

63.

63.

Ehon Mushi Erami

(Picture book of selected insects)

Kitagawa Utamaro (1754–1806)

1788, Edo period

Two volumes; printed in ink, colors, and gold on paper

H 27 W 18.4 (each)

CBJ No. 1675 (141)

One of the most celebrated picture books of its kind, this anthology of *kyōka* (humorous poems) was compiled by Yadoya no Meshimori and contains fifteen double-page spreads of illustrations by Utamaro. Each illustration depicts two different insects or reptiles among grass and flowers, and is accompanied by a pair of *kyōka* relating to the illustration. Subtle in coloring, the pictures are of exceptional quality.

Meticulous in detail, the illustrations nevertheless differ from scientific drawings of natural flora and fauna. Instead they represent a successful attempt at treating non-*ukiyo-e* subjects in a realistic manner. At the same time they challenge the more stereotyped scientific studies of these very subjects.

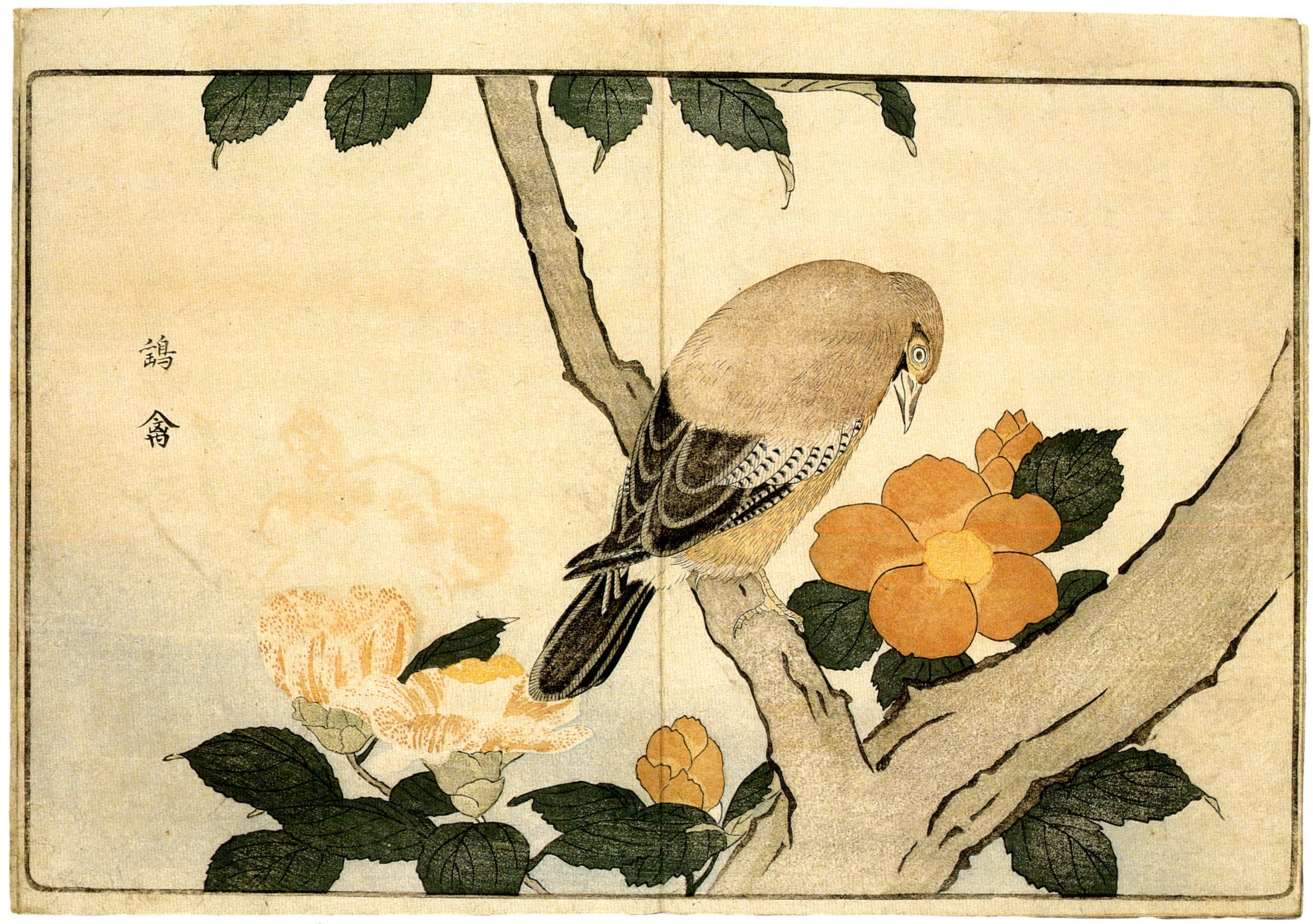

64.

64.

Kaihaku Raikin Zui

(Pictures of imported birds)

Kitao Masayoshi (1764–1824)

1790, Edo period

One volume; printed in ink and colors on paper

H 25.5 W 18.7

CBJ No. 1632 (144)

Rare imported birds that had been brought to Nagasaki by the Chinese and Dutch form the subject of this picture book. According to the colophon, the drawings were the work of the Chinese residents of Nagasaki and were selected by Seki Eibun. The twelve illustrations were copies for the engraving by Kitao Masayoshi, whose studies of birds and plants exhibit a native adaptation of the Chinese style. These scenes owe nothing to *ukiyo-e* and are instead comparable with Utamaro's famous efforts in the same direction (cat. no. 63). Only in subject matter is there any similarity between the two artists, for the contrast between Utamaro's realistic approach and Masayoshi's adapted Chinese style is indeed great.

Although this particular volume is certainly one of the early copies of the first edition, the existence of another fine copy (in the Kobe City Museum), which was printed with an extra color block on one of the illustrations, indicates that the Chester Beatty copy was produced somewhat later.[17]

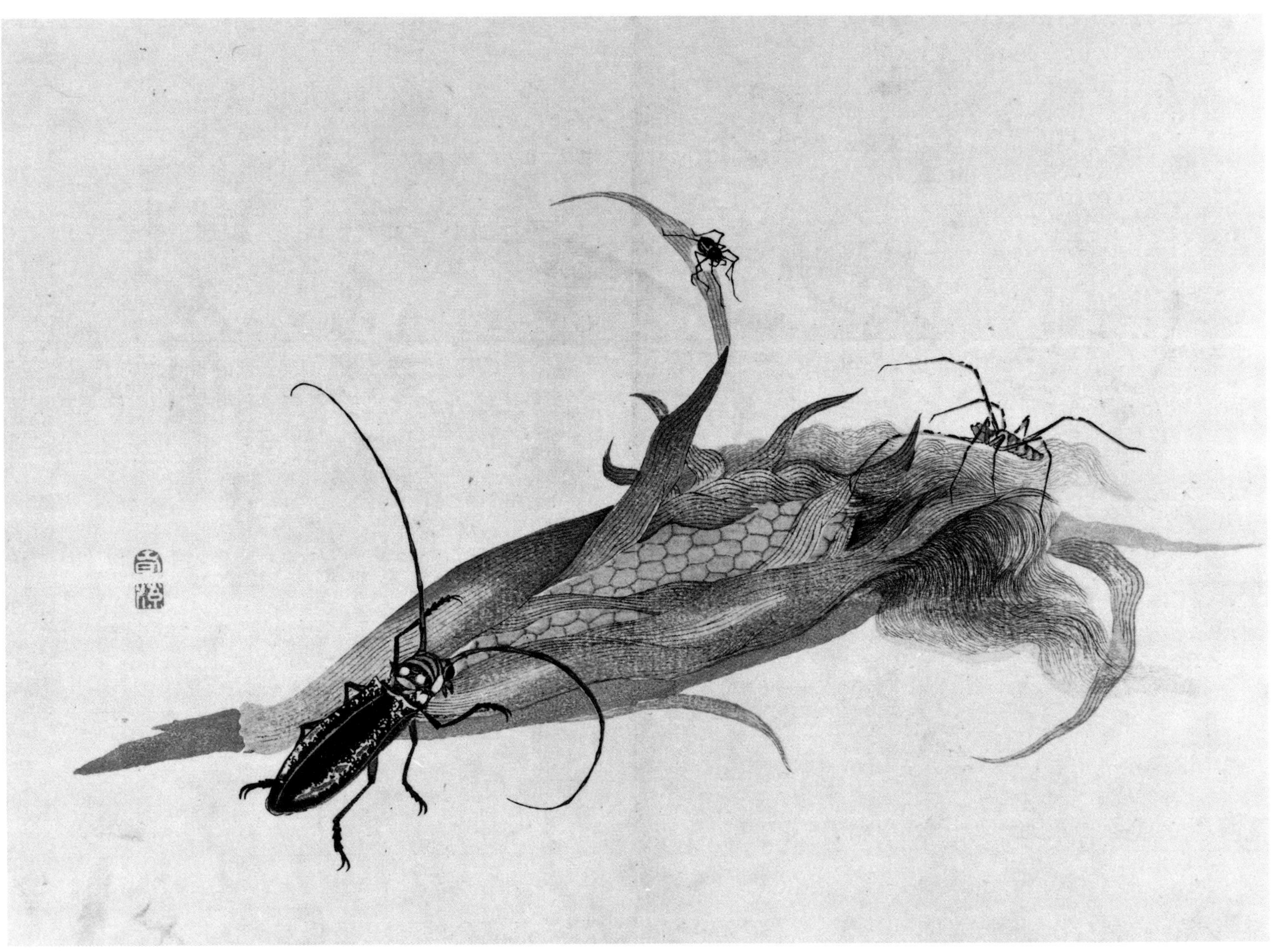

65.

65.

Chūka Senzen

(Illustrated book of plants and insects)

Mori Shunkei (fl. 1800–1820)

1820, Edo period

One volume; printed in ink and colors on paper

H 20.7 W 14.2

CBJ No. 1677 (172)

These twelve double-page illustrations of plants and insects are realistic studies by Mori Shunkei and may have been influenced by Utamaro's book of insects (cat. no. 63). This is a fine copy of the first edition, engraved and printed by Tani Seikō.

Notes

1 The Tosa school, founded by Tosa Yukihino, was a leading practitioner of *yamato-e,* particularly in the Edo period. Unlike the Kanō school, which was mainly supported by the samurai class, the Tosa school was given the title *edokoro,* due to its favor at court. The Sumiyoshi school was founded by Sumiyoshi Jokei, a student of the Tosa school.

2 Murase Miyeko, *Tales of Japan* (New York: Oxford University Press, 1986), p. 113.

3 Sorimachi Shigeo (1901–1991) was a rare book dealer and a renowned collector. In 1979, he offered his work and financial assistance to help publish a catalogue of the Chester Beatty Library collection of Japanese paintings. He privately published one thousand copies.

4 *Hokkyō* was originally one of the rankings of Buddhist priests or monks. During the Buke (Bakufu) period, the great honor of the title was also given to a distinguished medical doctor, painter, or craftsman.

5 Sakakibara Satoru, *"Suntory Bijutsukan Ronshuu,"* no. 3 (Tokyo, 1989), p. 81.

6 Murase, *Tales of Japan,* p. 81.

7 Asahara Yoshiko, "Yoshitsune Jigokuyaburi o megutte," in *Kokubun Mejiro,* no. 22 (1983), pp. 123–31.

[8] One example is in the Suntory Museum Collection in Tokyo. See Sakakibara Satoru, "Suntory Bijutsukanbon 'Shutendōji Emaki' o megutte" (Shutendōji Emaki owned by the Suntory Museum of Art), in *Kokka* 1076 (part I), pp. 7–26, and *Kokka* 1077 (part II), pp. 33–61 (1984). Also see Satake Akihiro, *Shuten Dōji Ibun,* no. 55 (Tokyo: Heibonsha Sensho, 1977).

[9] See James T. Araki, "Otogi-zōshi and Nara-ehon," in *Monumenta Nipponica* 36, no. 1 (Spring 1981), pp. 2–3.

[10] Matsumoto Ryūshin, *Zaigai Nara-ehon* (Tokyo: Kadokawa Publishing Company, 1981), p. 22.

[11] For a translation see James T. Araki, "Bunshō Sōshi: The Tale of Bunshō, the salt-maker," in *Monumenta Nipponica* 38, no. 3 (Autumn 1983).

[12] Tsuji Nobuo, *Zaigai Nara-ehon* (Tokyo: Kadokawa Publishing Company, 1981), pp. 39–40.

[13] Asahara Yoshiko, "Zaigai 'Mai no Hon' o megutte," in *Nihon Joshidaigaku Kiyō,* no. 33 (1984), pp. 7–8.

[14] Wakisaka Atsushi, "Chogonka Emaki Ko," in *Nihon Bijutsu Kōgei* 6–62 (1990), pp. 11–17.

[15] Sakakibara Satoru, "Sumiyoshi Jokei's 'Tohi No Zukan' Kaidai," in *Kobijutsu,* no. 88 (Tokyo, 1988), pp. 48–75.

[16] Aiso Kazuhiro, *Kenkyūkiyō,* no. 22 (Osaka: Osaka City Museum, 1990), pp. 43–55.

[17] This minute yet significant difference between the two copies was discovered by Mr. Narusawa of the Kobe City Museum in 1988 during the Chester Beatty Library exhibition in Japan.

Bibliography

Aiso Kazuhiro. *Kenkyūkiyō*, no. 22. Osaka: Osaka City Museum, 1990.

Araki, James T. "Bunshō Sōshi: The Tale of Bunshō, the salt-maker." *Monumenta Nipponica* 38, no. 3 (Autumn 1983).

_________. "Otogi-zōshi and Nara-ehon." *Monumenta Nipponica* 36, no. 1 (Spring 1981): 2–3.

Asahara Yoshiko. "Yoshitsune Jigokuyaburi o megutte." *Kokubun Mejiro,* no. 22 (1983): 123–31.

_________. "Zaigai 'Mai no Hon' o megutte." *Nihon Joshidaigaku Kiyō,* no. 38 (1984): 7–8.

Kennedy, Brian. *Alfred Chester Beatty and Ireland, 1950-1968.* Dublin: Glendale Press, 1988.

Keyes, Roger. *The Art of Surimono.* London: Sotheby's, 1985.

Murase Miyeko. *Tales of Japan.* New York: Oxford University Press, 1986.

Matsumoto Ryūshin. *Zaigai Nara-ehon.* Tokyo: Kadokawa Publishing Company, 1981.

Sakakibara Satoru. "Sumiyoshi Jokei's 'Tohi No Zukan' Kaidai." *Kobijutsu,* no. 88 (Tokyo, 1988): 48–75.

_________. *"Suntory Bijutsukan Ronshū,"* no. 3 (Tokyo, 1989).

_________. "Suntory Bijutsukanbon 'Shutendōji Emaki' o megutte" (Shutendōji Emaki owned by the Suntory Museum of Art). *Kokka* 1076 (part I, 1984): 7–26; and *Kokka* 1077 (part II, 1984): 33–61.

Satake Akihiro. *Shuten Dōji Ibun,* no. 55. Tokyo: Heibonsha Sensho, 1977.

Tsuji Nobuo. *Zaigai Nara-ehon.* Tokyo: Kadokawa Publishing Company, 1981.

Ushioda Yoshiko. *Nihon no Monogatari-e* (Chester Beatty Collection: Tales of Japan). Tokyo: Suntory Museum of Art, 1988.

Wakisaka Atsushi. "Chogōnka Emaki Kō." *Nihon Bujutsu Kōgei* 6–62 (1990): 11–17.